Kids
in
the Kitchen

by Linda K. Shriberg
and Carole Nicholas

Illustrated by Robert Cavey

WANDERER BOOKS
NEW YORK

Copyright © 1980 by Linda K. Shriberg and Carole Nicholas
All rights reserved
including the right of reproduction
in whole or in part in any form
Published by Wanderer Books
A Simon & Schuster Division of
Gulf & Western Corporation
Simon & Schuster Building
1230 Avenue of the Americas
New York, New York 10020

Designed by Irving Perkins
Manufactured in the United States of America
10 9 8 7 6 5 4 3 2 1

Wanderer and colophon are trademarks
of Simon & Schuster

Library of Congress Cataloging in Publication Data

Shriberg, Linda K
Kids in the kitchen.

Includes index.
SUMMARY: Recipes for 21 menus with "time-locked"
schedules so that everything is ready at once.
1. Cookery—Juvenile literature. [1. Cookery]
I. Nicholas, Carole, joint author. II. Cavey, Robert.
III. Title.

TX652.5.S53   641.5   79–24592

ISBN 0–671–33023–3

To our families
Larry, Liz, Kathy, Jan
and
Bob, Scott, and Paul

Contents

Foreword

Kids in the Kitchen is an ideal cookbook for the young cook who has outgrown the "package mix" and "heat-and-serve convenience food" phase. It provides nutritious dinner menus with coordinated recipes as well as unique time-locked preparation plans so all the dishes are cooked and ready to serve at the same time.

The foods used in the recipes are readily available in most local food stores. As an extra, menus are planned so that dieters can easily modify them by substituting fresh fruit for the richer desserts and by reducing the portion size of the other foods served.

In addition, the menus and recipes were put to the real test. Young cooks actually prepared the menus and recipes without the help of an adult. The feedback on directions, timing, and taste acceptance from these cooks, as well as from other family members, was carefully considered and revisions were made. The revised recipes were then prepared by a different group of young cooks.

Kids in the Kitchen is the cookbook young cooks can understand and enjoy!

Adeline Garner Shell
Food Editor
Consumer Education Specialist

Preface

Kids in the Kitchen is a unique book. There are few teenage cookbooks that emphasize complete dinner menus; there certainly are no such books that are as practical and as pleasurable to read as this one by Linda Shriberg and Carole Nicholas.

In every way, this book is built on a solid foundation. The experiences and abilities of the authors are apparent. As classroom teachers, reading specialists, careful writers and researchers, and as mothers, they are highly qualified to write a cookbook that is technically sound and that can be understood and enjoyed by everyone.

Ultimately, a cookbook is only as good as its recipes. As the father of two teenage daughters and the husband of a nurse who often works the "p.m. shift," I am delighted with this one. The menus are complete, nutritious, and easy on the budget. *Kids in the Kitchen* will be used and enjoyed by our family as well as by many others, I'm sure.

Dale D. Johnson, Ph.D.
Professor of Education
University of Wisconsin

Acknowledgments

We wish to thank the following "chefs"—our husbands, and all the teenagers—who piloted the menus in this book:

Leah Blum   Julie Rich
Jessica Dropsho   Elizabeth Shriberg
Kirsten Johnson   Kathy Shriberg
Karen Kiemel   Larry Shriberg
Susie Liddicoat   Christy Vedejs
Bob Nicholas   Julie Wehlage

Their suggestions about the meals as well as the wording of the directions and the timing of the recipes have been invaluable to us in creating a handbook that new cooks can understand and enjoy.

Introduction

Everyone cooks nowadays! Homemakers, career people, husbands, wives, bachelors—everyone needs to have some skills in the kitchen for today's life-styles. Look at the rows and rows of cookbooks in bookstores; you can buy a cookbook for just about every imaginable type of cooking. But this one is different. Here's why.

This Cookbook Is for You

This cookbook is for teenagers. Here's what it contains:
- *Complete dinners.* With mothers working more, and the increase in single-parent families, you can really help by cooking some evening dinners. Not just an occasional pizza or a nice dessert, but complete, delicious meals.
- *Inexpensive, nutritious dinners.* The dinners you'll cook are priced within the average budget for a family of six. These dinners are made with basic, wholesome foods, and provide generous portions. Moreover, all ingredients are available in supermarkets throughout the United States and Canada.
- *Step-by-step dinners.* If you're new to the kitchen, you'll

especially appreciate the step-by-step instructions for each dinner. The instructions should be clear enough for you to follow without help from Mom, Dad, or any other experienced cook.

· *Time-efficient dinners.* Cooking is fun, but who wants to spend all afternoon fixing the evening meal! Our dinners usually require one to one and one-half hours from start to finish. A few of the dinners take as long as two and one-half hours; however, you almost always get a break while things are cooking. Just follow the time-locked preparation plan—everything has been carefully coordinated for the most efficient use of your time.

Here's How to Use the Book

Kids in the Kitchen consists of twenty-one delicious dinner menus. They're not arranged in any particular order, so you can start with any meal that suits your mood. Each meal has these features:

INTRODUCTION

Every dinner has a name that sets an overall theme for the individual recipes. Most include historical information or humorous tidbits about your dinner. You can really impress your family and friends by casually dropping a fact here and there as you serve each delicious dish.

RECIPES

Most of the menus in *Kids in the Kitchen* have four recipes:
1. A main dish of meat, poultry, or fish
2. A starch, such as potatoes, rice, or pasta
3. A vegetable or salad
4. A dessert

As a rule, hors d'oeuvres, relishes, and condiments are not included, although they are sometimes suggested. Of course, the meals may be supplemented according to family tastes. If a family desires rolls and honey with every dinner, or a dish of pickles and olives, by all means, add them. Beverages, too, are left up to individual preferences.

All meals in *Kids in the Kitchen* are well balanced for nutrition. They also satisfy three important principles of meal planning: *taste, color,* and *texture*.

Taste. Achieving the right combination of taste requires that a food with a distinctive taste be accompanied by foods of countertastes. For example, fish is considered to have a salty taste; serving tart lemon wedges with fish provides a nice countertaste. Watch for this principle in these menus and in your own meal planning. Notice how in Mexicali Dinner, for example, you serve a cold, refreshing lemon-mint dessert after the hot Taco Bowl main dish.

Color. Foods of different colors add interest to any meal. Imagine how drab a dinner of creamed chicken, white rice, cauliflower, and vanilla ice cream would be. Often it's difficult to make every dish in the meal a different color, but some variation surely is needed. In Count Your Chickens Dinner, for example, we include golden brown chicken, yellow corn pudding, green broccoli, and a bright red dessert.

Texture. Texture is the third principle of meal planning that will add appeal to your dinner. Texture is often overlooked, even when taste and color are carefully considered, but the textures of the food you serve should be varied. A smooth food, for example, should be accompanied by at least one food of a granular or crunchy texture. Sorry, Charlie! Dinner balances texture in this way: the main dish is a creamy casserole, so it's served with crisp baked carrots and a wheel of crunchy garden vegetables.

Finally, a statement about words printed in italics that you'll come across in the recipe directions. These words are cooking terms and are defined or explained in the Glossary, beginning on page 131. We have tried to be precise; for best results, be sure to follow all procedural terms exactly as written.

TIME-LOCKED PREPARATION PLAN

Success in preparing and serving any dinner requires the right timing. If you follow our unique time-locked preparation plan, you can be sure that the dishes in your dinner will be ready to serve at the proper time. Let's see how this plan works for each dinner.

A sentence at the top of each timetable tells you how far in advance to begin dinner. If everyone is going to be ready to eat at six o'clock, for example, and if the sentence says that dinner must be started one hour and forty-five minutes earlier, you'll need to be in the kitchen at 4:15. As you'll see, though, you probably won't be working the full hour and forty-five minutes. In fact, usually you'll have one or more breaktimes away from the kitchen.

Probably the best way to explain how the time-locked preparation plans work is by using one example. Take a few minutes to look over the recipes and timetables in Count Your Chickens Dinner, pages 3–8. Then follow the play-by-play directions below to see how the four recipes in this dinner are coordinated:

- Start with Phase I on the timetable. Phase I tells you to do Steps 1–6 of the kisel. This phase has you prepare the gelatin-based dessert early, so that it will have time to set in the refrigerator. Go on to Phase II.
- Phase II has you prepare the corn pudding (Steps 2–8) just to the point before baking. Go on to Phase III.
- Phase III instructs you to preheat the oven and to prepare the chicken through Step 5. (Note that the oven is turned on just long enough to preheat, in order to avoid wasting gas or electricity.) Go on to Phase IV.
- Phase IV has you place both the corn pudding and the chicken in the preheated oven for the same amount of cooking time (one hour). You can now enjoy a forty-five-minute breaktime away from the kitchen.
- When you return to the kitchen after breaktime, begin Phase V, preparing the broccoli from start to finish (Steps 1–9). This will take about fifteen minutes—just when the corn pudding and chicken should be ready. Go on to Phase VI.

· Phase VI tells you to take the corn pudding (Step 10) and the chicken (Step 7) from the oven. The broccoli is also ready to be served. Now you can join your family and friends at the dinner table and enjoy a superb dinner. Then, after the main course, go on to Phase VII.
· Phase VII has you serving the kisel dessert, which is now set. Happy eating!

A Last Word

The ultimate goal of *Kids in the Kitchen* is to help you learn how to coordinate recipes from a variety of menus. When you first begin cooking dinners, you'll probably feel more confident if you follow our menus exactly. But, in time, we hope you'll experiment with different combinations of recipes. The chicken dish in Count Your Chickens Dinner does not always have to be served with corn pudding, broccoli, and kisel. Try substituting scalloped potatoes from First Chop Dinner for the corn pudding. Both the corn and the potatoes require a 350°F oven, although the potatoes need an extra ten minutes of baking time. Just put the potatoes in the oven before preparing the chicken. Then, when the chicken is prepared and ready for the oven (ten minutes later), both dishes will require the same hour of baking time.

Eventually, you might want to alter some of the ingredients. Combine favorite herbs in meat and vegetable dishes, create toppings for desserts, place additional vegetables in salads. . . .

As with anything else, practice in preparing meals will bring proficiency. And with proficiency, we hope you'll experience the satisfaction of having learned a valuable skill and the joy of tasty and nutritious cooking.

Kids
in the
the Kitchen
Dinners

"Count Your Chickens" Dinner

Serves 6

You certainly can count your chickens with this menu, because the recipes are almost foolproof and bound to come out winners.

Although you'll have to plan on about one hour and forty-five minutes from the time you begin until dinnertime, almost all the preparations take place during the first forty minutes. So, while the kisel is setting in the refrigerator, and the chicken and corn pudding are baking together in the oven, you can enjoy a forty-five minute breaktime. Use this opportunity to read the newspaper, walk the dog, or shampoo your hair. Then, return to the kitchen in time to prepare the Tangy Broccoli. With good planning, it should be crisp and ready to serve just when you're taking the Good 'n' Easy Chicken and the Ritzy Corn Pudding out of the oven.

Good 'n' Easy Chicken
Ritzy Corn Pudding   Tangy Broccoli
Cranberry-Raspberry Kisel

3

Good 'n' Easy Chicken

This dish is likely to become a family favorite because it is so good and so easy. Vary the seasonings according to your family's tastes. We like to sprinkle garlic salt on our chicken. Consider trying tarragon, poultry seasoning, or lemon zest.

    3 whole chicken breasts, split (6 halves)
      salt
      pepper
      paprika
    3 tablespoons butter or margarine

1. Preheat the oven to 350°F.
2. Rinse the chicken breasts under cold water. Pat dry with paper towels.
3. Place the chicken breasts on a cookie sheet or in a shallow baking dish. *Season* lightly on both sides with salt and pepper.
4. Turn the breasts skin side up, and sprinkle the tops moderately with paprika.
5. Divide the butter into six equal slices. Place a butter slice on each chicken breast.
6. *Bake* for 1 hour, or until *fork-tender.* (The skin should be crisp.)
7. Using potholders, carefully remove the pan of chicken breasts from the oven. With a slotted spatula, transfer the breasts to a serving platter.

Ritzy Corn Pudding

This recipe serves 8, but don't count on leftovers!

        1 tablespoon butter or margarine
   3 or 4 green onions (scallions)
      ¼ cup (½ stick) butter or margarine
      3 eggs, medium size or larger
      1 can (7 ounces) whole kernel corn
    36 Ritz-type crackers
      1 can (17 ounces) cream-style corn

    1 cup milk
    1 teaspoon salt

1. Preheat the oven to 350°F.
2. Using the 1 tablespoon butter, *grease* a 1½-quart casserole.
3. *Slice* off the root ends of the green onions. Remove any dried or wilted outer leaves. With a paring knife (or with kitchen scissors), finely slice both the white and green parts of the onions.
4. *Melt* the ¼ cup butter in a small skillet over low heat. Add the sliced green onions and *sauté* until tender.
5. Break the eggs into a large bowl. *Beat* slightly with a fork or wire whisk.
6. *Drain* the 7-ounce can of whole kernel corn in a colander or strainer. Place the drained corn in the large bowl with the eggs.
7. Using your hands, crumble the crackers over the egg-corn mixture. (The crumbs can be large and coarse.)
8. Add the sautéed onions, the entire (undrained) 17-ounce can of cream-style corn, the milk, and the salt to the egg-corn-cracker mixture. *Stir* well. Pour the mixture into the greased casserole.
9. *Bake* uncovered until firm (about 1 hour).
10. Using potholders, carefully remove the casserole from the oven and set on a trivet or warming pad.

Tangy Broccoli

Preparing fresh broccoli involves a little bit of work, but the result is delicious, tender-crisp broccoli. Our special method of cooking and steaming keeps the vitamins sealed in and not lost in a water bath.

        1 large bunch fresh broccoli*
        1 teaspoon salt
    2 to 3 tablespoons butter or margarine
        1 lemon
          salt

* If fresh broccoli is not available, substitute two 10-ounce packages of frozen broccoli spears. Follow package directions for cooking and draining; then proceed with Step 8.

1. Place the broccoli in a large bowl and cover with cold water.
2. Select a large pot with a lid and with sides at least 4½ inches high. Fill the pot with 1 inch of water and 1 teaspoon salt. Bring to a *rapid boil* over high heat.
3. While the water is reaching a boil, prepare the broccoli: remove the broccoli from the bowl of water and rinse several times under cold running water (bugs sometimes hide in the broccoli "flowers").
4. With a sharp knife, *cut* the stalk ends of the broccoli so that the height of the broccoli is just slightly shorter than the sides of the pot. (The broccoli is going to stand upright to cook.) Now *peel* off the thick outer skin of the stalks up to the "flowers" (a vegetable peeler does this very nicely).
5. Tear off about 8 to 10 inches of aluminum foil, and fold it lengthwise several times to make a band approximately 2 inches wide. Secure the band around the broccoli bunch just under the "flowers."
6. When the water has reached a rapid boil, carefully place the broccoli upright in the pot. Cover with the lid. Lower the heat, and *simmer* 15 to 20 minutes or until the broccoli stalks are *fork-tender*. (Do not overcook, or your broccoli will be mushy. The trick in preparing perfect broccoli is to cook it just long enough to retain its crispness.)
7. Carefully remove the lid. Using two large forks or kitchen

Foil band should be secured tightly under broccoli flowers.

tongs, carefully lift the broccoli from the pot and transfer it to a colander to *drain*. Remove the foil band.

8. Place the drained broccoli in a serving dish. Top the broccoli with the butter. As the butter melts, use a fork to gently turn the broccoli to coat.

9. Cutting in the *lengthwise* direction only, divide the lemon in half with a paring knife. Then divide each half into thirds. Arrange the 6 lemon wedges around the broccoli. The lemon will give the broccoli a real tang. (Each diner may squeeze to taste.) Sprinkle with salt to taste.

Cranberry-Raspberry Kisel

Truly a dessert from Russia, with love.

    1 package unflavored gelatin (or 1 tablespoon unflavored gelatin)
    ¼ cup cold water
    2 cups cranberry juice cocktail
    1 package (10 ounces) frozen raspberries (do not defrost!)
       whipped topping (or ½ cup heavy cream, whipped)

1. In a small dish, *stir* the gelatin into the water (granules will remain).
2. Using a medium saucepan over high heat, bring 1 cup of the cranberry juice cocktail to a *boil*. Then immediately remove the saucepan from the heat.
3. Add the gelatin-water mixture to the hot cranberry juice cocktail and stir until the gelatin is *dissolved*.
4. Add the remaining 1 cup of cold cranberry juice cocktail.
5. Add the frozen raspberries to the cranberry liquid. Stir with a fork to break the raspberries apart. (This step will take several minutes.)
6. Divide the kisel among 6 dessert bowls, and refrigerate until set, about 1 hour and 45 minutes.
7. At serving time, spoon whipped topping over each dish of kisel.

"COUNT YOUR CHICKENS" DINNER

Start Phase I about 1 hour and 45 minutes before dinnertime.

Phase	Good 'n' Easy Chicken	Ritzy Corn Pudding	Tangy Broccoli	Cranberry-Raspberry Kisel
I				Steps 1–6
II		Steps 2–8		
III	Steps 1–5			
IV	Step 6	Step 9		
45-MINUTE BREAKTIME				
V			Steps 1–9	
VI	Step 7	Step 10		
VII				At dessert time, Step 7

"Sole Food" Dinner

Serves 6

It is nutritionally sound to include at least one fish dinner when you plan your weekly menu. So, in fishing through our bulging files, we were hooked by an old family favorite: Sole-Satisfying Fillets.

An old wives' tale, based partly on fears of choking on a bone, says to always include potatoes or rice with any fish dish. We went angling deep in our files and caught a winner with Neptune's Rice. You'll have only to reel in the Beets 'n' Orange and The Captain's Favorite Chocolate Cake to boast a seaworthy menu.

Start preparations about two hours before dinner, but plan on being in the kitchen for only half that time. If you live beside a lake, consider using your forty-five-minute breaktime to do some speedy fishing. Later, you'll have another, shorter breaktime to mull over some fish facts:

- There are at least twenty-five thousand species of fish.
- Raising fish in hatcheries can be traced back to the ancient Chinese. After the fall of the Roman Empire, fish culture disappeared until the eighteenth century.

9

· The elephant-nose mormyrid produces an electric field to warn of approaching danger and to help locate food.
· The male sea horse carries the eggs in his pouch until they are ready to be expelled.
· The blue whale is the largest animal in the world. It may be one hundred feet long and weigh up to one hundred fifty tons.

Plan to serve Sole Food Dinner to your family and friends often. We guarantee they'll fall for it hook, line, and sinker every time!

Sole-Satisfying Fillets
Neptune's Rice   *Beets 'n' Orange*
The Captain's Favorite Chocolate Cake

Sole-Satisfying Fillets

The term *sole* pertains to the Soleidae family of flatfish, noted for their small mouths and tiny, close-set eyes. Sole fillets are highly esteemed in Europe and America as table food and comprise some relatives of the flounder family. The name comes from the Latin *solea,* meaning *sandal:* if you look at a picture of a soleoid fish, you will see that it resembles the flat shape of the sole of the foot.

> ½ cup (1 stick) butter or margarine
> 1 lemon
>   several sprigs fresh parsley
> 2 green onions (scallions)
> 1 to 1½ teaspoons salt
> ½ teaspoon rosemary leaves (don't skip this!)
> 2½ pounds (approx.) fresh sole fillets (or use frozen fillets, thawed)

1. Preheat the oven to 350°F.
2. Place the butter in a small saucepan.
3. On a cutting board, using a sharp knife, *cut* the lemon in half *crosswise.* Cut one of the lemon halves into 6 equal wedges. Cover the wedges with plastic wrap and refrigerate until serving time.

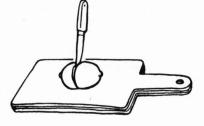

Lemon halves for wedges or juice in Sole-Satisfying Fillets.

4. Squeeze the juice from the remaining lemon half. Remove any seeds from the juice. Pour the juice into the saucepan with the butter.

5. Rinse the parsley under cold water. Shake off any excess water. On a cutting board, use a paring knife (or kitchen scissors) to *mince* the parsley. Add the minced parsley to the butter and lemon juice.

6. *Slice* off the root ends of the green onions. Remove any dry or wilted outer leaves. Use the paring knife (or kitchen scissors) to thinly slice both the white and green parts of the onions. Add the onion slices, along with the salt and rosemary, to the ingredients in the saucepan.

7. Over medium-low heat, warm the contents of the saucepan just until the butter *melts. Stir* occasionally to combine ingredients.

8. Rinse the sole fillets under cold water. Pat dry with paper towels.

9. Pour half the melted butter mixture into a baking dish approximately 13 inches by 9 inches.

10. Arrange the sole fillets in a single layer (overlap slightly, if necessary) on top of the melted butter in the baking dish.

Pour the remaining half of the butter mixture over the fillets.

11. *Bake* uncovered for 30 to 35 minutes, or until the fish flakes easily when touched with a fork.

12. Using potholders, carefully remove the baking dish from the oven and set on warming pads on the dining table.

13. Remove the 6 lemon wedges from the refrigerator and arrange around the fish. Use a wide spatula to transfer the fillets to dinner plates. Be sure to top the fillets with generous spoonfuls of herb-butter sauce.

Neptune's Rice

Green peas and cashew nuts make this rice dish colorful and crunchy.

2½ cups water
1 cup raw converted rice
2 chicken bouillon cubes
1 tablespoon butter or margarine
⅓ cup (from a 10-ounce package) frozen green peas
½ cup cashews (or substitute almonds, whole or slivered, if cashews are not available)

1. In a medium saucepan that has a tight-fitting lid, bring the water to a *rapid boil* over high heat.

2. *Stir* in the rice, bouillon cubes, and butter.

3. Cover the saucepan with the lid. Reduce the heat to low, and *simmer* for 15 minutes.

4. Break off enough peas from the block of frozen peas to fill about ⅓ cup. (Store the remaining peas in the freezer for another meal—Snappy Stew, page 17, for example.) Add the ⅓ cup peas to the simmering rice. Cover the saucepan again and continue to simmer for about 10 minutes more (or until all the water is absorbed by the rice).

5. Add the cashews to the rice and peas and stir gently to combine ingredients.

6. Transfer the rice mixture to a serving dish.

Beets 'n' Orange

A tribute to the French, who first combined beets with fresh orange.

    1 orange
    2 cans (16 ounces each) sliced beets
       salt to taste

1. *Grate* enough orange rind to equal 2 teaspoons. Set aside.
2. *Cut* the orange in half and squeeze the juice from one of the halves into a small dish. Set aside. (Store the other orange half in plastic wrap in the refrigerator to eat as a healthy snack or to use in a fresh fruit salad.)
3. Pour the beets and their liquid into a medium saucepan and warm over medium heat.
4. *Drain* the heated beets in a colander or strainer. Place the beets in a serving dish.
5. Add the reserved orange juice and rind to the beets. *Stir* gently to coat all the beet slices.

The Captain's Favorite Chocolate Cake

This cake is delicious served warm with a scoop of vanilla ice cream.

    1 tablespoon shortening
       flour
    1 package (about 18½ ounces) deep chocolate or extra dark chocolate cake mix
    1 package (4½ ounces) chocolate fudge or deep chocolate instant pudding mix
    4 eggs, medium-size or larger (if you have small eggs, use 5)
    ¾ cup oil
    ¾ cup water
    1 cup (6 ounces) chocolate chips

1. Preheat the oven to 350°F.
2. *Grease* and *flour* a 10-inch tube pan or a large bundt pan.
3. Put all the ingredients except the chocolate chips into a large mixing bowl.
4. Using an electric mixer, *blend* the ingredients on low speed. Scrape the bowl and beaters with a rubber spatula to include any dry clumps.
5. *Beat* with the electric mixer on medium speed for 3 minutes. Scrape any excess batter from the beaters into the bowl.
6. Add the chocolate chips to the batter. *Stir* with a wooden spoon to combine.
7. Pour the batter into the prepared tube or bundt pan. Be sure to use a rubber spatula to scrape off any batter from the bowl.
8. *Bake* for 45 to 50 minutes, or until the cake is done. Insert a toothpick down into the cake. If the cake is done, the toothpick will come out clean. (Retest if you hit a chocolate chip.)
9. Using potholders, carefully remove the cake from the oven.
10. Cool the cake on a rack for about 15 to 20 minutes.
11. Place a serving plate on the top of the cake and carefully invert. Gently remove the cake pan. Allow the cake to continue to cool at room temperature.
12. *Slice* the cake. Serve warm or cooled.

"SOLE FOOD" DINNER

Start Phase I about 2 hours before dinnertime.

Phase	Sole-Satisfying Fillets	Neptune's Rice	Beets 'n' Orange	The Captain's Favorite Chocolate Cake
I				Steps 1–8
45-MINUTE BREAKTIME				
II				Steps 9–10
III	Steps 2–11			
IV				Step 11
V		Steps 1–3		
15-MINUTE BREAKTIME				
VI		Step 4		
VII			Steps 1–5	
VIII	Steps 12–13	Steps 5–6		
IX				At dessert time, Step 12

"It's a Snap" Dinner

Serves 6

Although you must allow two and a half hours from the time you begin until serving time, this dinner is a snap in terms of ease of preparations. The stew takes about a half hour to assemble; then it simmers for the two remaining hours, with just a few steps to do toward the end. Put the gelatin mixture needed for the dessert into the refrigerator to set, and you can enjoy a substantial one-hour breaktime for dusting the furniture, changing the linens, or listening to your favorite records. Then return to the kitchen to add fresh vegetables to the Snappy Stew, to complete the Luscious Lime Frost, and to prepare the Pear-a-dise Salad.

Snappy Stew is a favorite dish in our homes. We accompany it with a crusty French bread—marvelous for soaking up all that wonderful gravy. We're sure that your family, too, will snap at the chance to be served this delicious dinner often.

Snappy Stew
Pear-a-dise Salad
Luscious Lime Frost

Snappy Stew

"Cookies in the stew?" your family will say!

         2 pounds lean beef stew meat
         1 medium onion, or ½ cup frozen chopped onion
    2 to 3 tablespoons oil
         1 lemon
    6 to 8 gingersnap cookies
         2 cans (8 ounces each) tomato sauce
         1 cup water
         2 tablespoons brown sugar, *packed*
         4 carrots
         4 medium potatoes
         2 stalks celery
         1 package (10 ounces) frozen peas (optional)

1. If the beef is not already cut up, on a cutting board, using a sharp knife, *cut* it into 1½-inch cubes.
2. Use the sharp knife to trim the meat cubes of any visible fat.
3. If using fresh onion: on a cutting board, use a sharp knife to cut off the ends of the onion. *Peel* off the dry outer skin and discard the skin and the ends. Coarsely *chop* the onion.

Steps in chopping an onion.

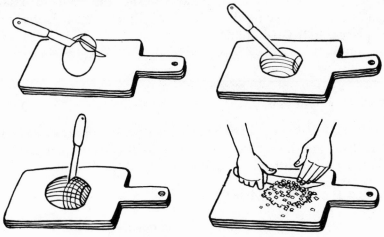

4. Heat the oil in a Dutch oven over medium-high heat until a drop of water splashed on the oil spatters.
5. Add the meat and onion to the hot oil. Toss gently with a wooden spoon until all sides of the beef cubes are nicely browned. (You are now *searing* the meat, or sealing in the meat juices.)
6. Cut the lemon in half and squeeze out the juice from both halves. Remove any seeds from the juice. Set the lemon juice aside.
7. Using your hands, *crumble* the gingersnaps directly into the Dutch oven. Don't worry if the crumbs are large; they will blend into the sauce.
8. Add the lemon juice, tomato sauce, water, and brown sugar to the Dutch oven, and *stir* until the mixture reaches a boil.
9. When the mixture reaches a boil, reduce the heat to medium-low. Cover the Dutch oven and *simmer* for 1¼ hours.
10. Peel the carrots and potatoes with a vegetable peeler. Remove the ends from the carrots with a sharp knife. Cut the carrots into 1-inch chunks. Quarter the potatoes.
11. Wash the celery, and remove the ends and leaves with a sharp knife. Cut the stalks into half-inch slices.
12. Add the carrots, potatoes, and celery to the stew mixture and simmer, covered, for 45 minutes. Set a timer.
13. If desired, 20 minutes before the timer is due to ring, add the frozen peas to the stew.
14. Using a large spoon or ladle, transfer the stew to a large casserole or serving dish. Or serve directly from Dutch oven placed on trivet on table.

Pear-a-dise Salad

The cream cheese–nut balls and the maraschino cherries make this salad true gourmet fare. For an equally delicious Pear-a-dise Salad, try substituting a granola-type cereal for the nuts.

     6 large lettuce leaves
     1 can (29 ounces) pear slices
     1 package (3 ounces) cream cheese

⅓ to ½ cup chopped walnuts or pecans (or any other nut of your choice)
maraschino cherries (optional)

1. Rinse the lettuce leaves with cold water. Gently pat dry with paper towels.
2. Place a lettuce leaf on each of 6 salad plates.
3. Lift out the pear slices from the can with a slotted spoon, and divide the slices evenly among the 6 salad plates. (Save the pear juice for a fruit drink, or use in a gelatin dish.)
4. Divide the cream cheese block into 12 equal parts. Using your hands, roll each cream cheese section into a ball.
5. Spread the nuts on a plate or on a piece of waxed paper. Roll each cream cheese ball in the nuts, until well coated.
6. Place 2 cream cheese–nut balls on each salad plate.
7. If desired, *garnish* the salad with maraschino cherries.
8. Store the salads in the refrigerator until serving time.
9. Remove salads from refrigerator and place on table.

Luscious Lime Frost

A light and refreshing dessert after a hearty meal.

1 cup boiling water
1 package (3 ounces) lime gelatin
8 or 9 ice cubes
1 lime
1½ cups vanilla ice cream, slightly softened
whipped topping

1. In a large bowl, combine the gelatin and boiling water, and *stir* until the gelatin is completely *dissolved.*
2. Add the ice cubes. Stir until the gelatin thickens and the ice cubes are almost melted. Remove any unmelted chips.
3. Pour the gelatin mixture into a 13-by-9-inch pan and refrigerate until set. (The large surface of the pan will speed up the setting process.)
4. *Cut* the lime in half *crosswise.* Squeeze the juice from one half only and pour the juice into a blender container, making sure to

remove any seeds. Cut the remaining lime half into 6 thin slices. Cover the slices with plastic wrap and refrigerate until Step 8.

5. Spoon the set lime gelatin into the blender container with the lime juice. Add the ice cream.

6. *Blend* on high speed until the mixture begins to thicken evenly.

7. Pour the blender mixture into 6 custard cups or small dessert bowls. Store in the refrigerator until serving time.

8. At serving time, *garnish* each dessert with a spoonful of whipped topping and a fresh lime slice.

"IT'S A SNAP" DINNER

Start Phase I about 2½ hours before dinnertime.

Phase	Snappy Stew	Pear-a-dise Salad	Luscious Lime Frost
I	Steps 1–9		
II			Steps 1–3
1-HOUR BREAKTIME			
III	Steps 10–12		
IV			Steps 4–7
V		Steps 1–8	
VI	Step 13 (optional)		
VII	Step 14	Step 9	
VIII			At dessert time, Step 8

"Harvest Festival" Dinner

Serves 6

Everyone loves a festival; and each autumn it's festival time for the farmer. It's the end of work in the fields and time to eat of the harvest. Harvest Festival Dinner is in keeping with this tradition.

Whether from your own or a friend's home garden, your local farmers' market, or the supermarket, September and October offer a cornucopia of fresh produce from the fields. Many of these fruits and vegetables are featured in our dinner tonight. The Fish or Fowl Squash Casserole is full of yellow or zucchini squash. Harvesters' Spinach Toss is a salad of fresh spinach leaves, cherry tomatoes, and green onions. And for dessert, there's a seasonal favorite: Autumnal Baked Apples. A dish of cold, tart cranberry sauce complements the meal nicely, along with warm buns and honey.

Begin preparations about one hour and fifteen minutes before eating. If you work efficiently, you'll earn a short, ten-minute breaktime—just long enough to arrange some gourds on dry oak or maple leaves for a centerpiece for the dining table.

If you want the folks at your house to reap the bounty of the fields, plan to make the hearty Harvest Festival Dinner a regular this autumn.

Fish or Fowl Squash Casserole
Harvesters' Spinach Toss
Autumnal Baked Apples

Fish or Fowl Squash Casserole

We suggest shellfish here, but 2 cans (about 7 ounces each) of the more economical tuna fish can be substituted. A delicious variation is to use 2 cups of cooked turkey or chicken in place of the fish.

 1 quart water (approx.)
 1 teaspoon salt
 2 pounds yellow summer squash or zucchini (or a combination of the two)
 1 small onion
 1 can (10½ ounces) cream of chicken soup
 1 cup dairy sour cream
 2 cups shrimp or crabmeat (or a combination of both), precooked or canned (or 2 cups cooked turkey or chicken)
½ cup (1 stick) butter or margarine
 1 package (about 8 ounces) herb-seasoned stuffing mix

1. Preheat the oven to 350°F.
2. In a large saucepan, bring the water and salt to a *rapid boil* over high heat.
3. While the water is reaching a boil, scrub the squash under cold water with a vegetable brush to remove any dirt. On a cutting board, use a sharp knife to *cut* off the ends from each piece of squash. Discard the ends; then cut the squash into ¼-inch slices.
4. Using the sharp knife, cut off both ends of the onion and discard. *Peel* off the dry outer skin from the onion. *Chop* the onion. (See diagram on page 17.)
5. Add the onion and squash to the boiling salted water. Con-

tinue boiling for 5 minutes. (If the water begins to boil over, reduce the heat slightly, but always maintain a boil.)

6. *Drain* the squash and onion thoroughly in a colander. Set aside until Step 8.
7. Combine the chicken soup and sour cream in a large bowl.
8. *Fold* the drained squash and onion into the creamed mixture. Add the shrimp and/or crabmeat (or the turkey or chicken). *Stir* gently.
9. *Melt* the butter in a large skillet over low heat, making sure it doesn't brown. When the butter is melted, empty the dry stuffing mix into the melted butter. Stir to combine.
10. Select a 2-quart baking dish or casserole and cover the bottom with half of the stuffing mixture.
11. Spoon the seafood- (or poultry-) squash mixture evenly over the stuffing. Top with the remaining stuffing mixture.
12. *Bake* uncovered for 30 minutes.
13. Using potholders, carefully remove the casserole from the oven. Set on hot pads or a trivet.

Harvesters' Spinach Toss

If fresh spinach isn't available, substitute romaine, chicory, or escarole.

> 1 pound fresh spinach
> 12 cherry tomatoes
> 2 green onions (scallions)
> salt and pepper to taste
> oil and vinegar dressing (your own or store-bought)

1. Rinse each spinach leaf under cold water to remove dirt. As you rinse, tear the spinach into bite-size pieces. Discard the stems and any bruised leaves. Place the torn spinach leaves in a colander or vegetable basket to *drain*. Remove any excess moisture by patting dry with paper towels. Transfer the spinach to a salad bowl.
2. Rinse the tomatoes under cold water. Remove any stems. Pat dry with paper towels. On a cutting board, use a sharp knife or

a paring knife to *cut* each tomato in half. Add the tomato halves to the spinach in the salad bowl.

3. Rinse the green onions with cold water. Pat dry with paper towels. Use the paring knife to cut off the root ends of the onions. Remove and discard any bruised or dried green skin. Thinly *slice* the onions, including both the white and green parts. Add the onion slices to the tomatoes and spinach.

4. Cover the salad bowl with plastic wrap and refrigerate until serving time.

5. At serving time, take the salad from the refrigerator. Remove the plastic wrap. Sprinkle the salad with salt and pepper. Toss gently. Place the salad bowl on the dining table and pass the oil and vinegar dressing.

Autumnal Baked Apples

Rome Beauty apples are considered best for baking, since the heavy skin helps them retain their shape. Other varieties for baking include Jonathan, Winesap, Newton, Greening.

    6 medium or large apples
    6 tablespoons brown sugar, *packed*
    3 tablespoons butter or margarine
      cinnamon and/or nutmeg
      optional: raisins, chopped nuts, cinnamon red hots, drained
      crushed pineapple or mincemeat
      water
      ice cream or whipped cream (optional)

1. Preheat the oven to 350°F.

2. Wash the apples with cold water. With a fork, prick the skin of each apple in four or five places to keep the skin from bursting.

3. *Core* the apples by using an apple corer in a circular motion down the length of the apple.

4. Arrange the apples right side up in a shallow baking dish or pie plate.

5. Fill each apple cavity with 1 tablespoon brown sugar, ½ table-

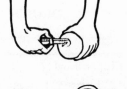

Using an apple corer to remove the cores from the apples.

   spoon butter, and a dash of cinnamon and/or nutmeg. Add any optional fillings.
6. Pour just enough water into the pan to cover the bottom.
7. *Bake* for 30 to 40 minutes, or until the apples are tender. (Cooking time varies considerably with the variety and size of the apples.) Test for doneness by piercing through the skin of the apple with a fork. The apples are done if the fruit under the skin is soft.
8. Using potholders, carefully remove the pan of apples from the oven and set the pan on a rack or trivet until dessert time. (This dessert is best when served warm.)
9. At dessert time, set one apple on each of 6 dessert plates. Spoon any pan syrup that has accumulated over the apples. Serve with ice cream or a dollop of whipped cream, if desired.

"HARVEST FESTIVAL" DINNER

Begin preparations about 1 hour and 15 minutes before dinnertime.

Phase	Fish or Fowl Squash Casserole	Harvesters' Spinach Toss	Autumnal Baked Apples
I			Steps 1–7
II	Steps 2–12		
III		Steps 1–4	
10-MINUTE BREAKTIME			
IV	Step 13		Step 8
V		Step 5	
VI			At dessert time, Step 9

"Trick or Treat" Dinner

Serves 6

In medieval times, the night before All Saints' Day was October 31. This night, called All Hallow's Eve, was later renamed Halloween.

In pagan days, October 31 marked the end of summer and the start of a new year. People thought the sun had been conquered by the dark: all the herds would return from pasture, laws would be renewed, and the souls of the dead would return to their homes. Even today, Mexicans visit grave sites to leave food for the dead. On All Hallow's Eve, it is still popularly believed that the dead will return to earth as witches, ghosts, black cats, or demons of any kind.

With the passing of time, Halloween has become quite secular. Nowadays, it is celebrated mainly by young children who wear costumes and go from house to house asking for a "trick or treat." Usually, the children disregard the tricks and collect the treats in the form of candy and other sweets. But in the nineteenth century, many tricks were played, causing extensive property damage—windows were broken, outhouses overturned. . . .

The original symbol of Halloween was the turnip. Later, the early immigrants to America used the pumpkin instead because it was more readily available. The tradition of carving the pumpkins grew, and candles were placed inside and lighted to ward off the evil spirits.

We feel we have prepared the perfect menu for your Halloween dinner. Don't let the ominous names of the recipes trick you, because you are in for a big treat with Crossbones Casserole, Green Toad Salad, and a relish plate of Broomsticks, Magic Wands, and Satan's Eyes. We suggest adding your favorite corn bread or dinner rolls to the main course. For dessert, we offer Hobgoblins' Mud Pie, a lovely concoction in orange and brown. Although you must start the meal about two hours and fifteen minutes before dinner, there is almost an hour off for a break. Use this time to carve a sinister face on your pumpkin or to put some finishing touches on your werewolf costume.

Happy trick or treating!

Crossbones Casserole
Green Toad Salad
Broomsticks, Magic Wands, and Satan's Eyes
Hobgoblins' Mud Pie

Crossbones Casserole

Fit for a skeleton!

  1 teaspoon butter or margarine
  3 quarts water
  1 tablespoon salt
  1 tablespoon oil
  3 cups uncooked elbow macaroni
  1 pound hot dogs
  4 ounces Cheddar cheese
  1 can (15 ounces) tomato sauce
½ teaspoon garlic salt
  2 tablespoons butter or margarine

1. Select a 2-quart casserole with a lid. *Grease* the casserole with the 1 teaspoon butter.

2. In a large pot, bring the water, salt, and oil to a *rapid boil* over a high heat.

3. Carefully add the dry macaroni. (If the water begins to boil over, reduce the heat, but always maintain a boil.)

4. Boil the macaroni for about 8 minutes or until the macaroni is *al dente*. *Stir* occasionally with a long-handled spoon to prevent the macaroni pieces from sticking together.

5. Preheat the oven to 350°F.

6. While the macaroni is cooking, take out a cutting board and a sharp knife. *Slice* all but 1 of the hot dogs into ½-inch rings. Set the 1 remaining hot dog aside until Step 12.

7. Use the sharp knife to *dice* the cheese.

8. *Drain* the macaroni in a colander. Then transfer the drained macaroni into the buttered casserole.

9. Add the hot dog slices, diced cheese, tomato sauce, and garlic salt to the macaroni. Stir well with a large spoon to combine ingredients.

10. *Dot* the macaroni mixture with the 2 tablespoons butter or margarine.

11. Cover the casserole and *bake* for 50 minutes.

12. *Cut* the 1 remaining hot dog in half *lengthwise*. Make a slit (about ½-inch long) at each end of the 2 hot dog pieces. Then cut 1 of the hot dog pieces in half *crosswise*. Using pot-

Cutting the hot dog to make the "crossbones."

holders, remove the casserole from the oven and uncover. Arrange the hot dog "bones" in an X-shape (see picture) on top of the baked macaroni. Return the uncovered casserole to the oven and bake for 10 minutes more.

13. Using potholders, remove the casserole from the oven and set on a hot pad or trivet.

Green Toad Salad

Even *people* will love this!

    1 can (20 ounces) crushed pineapple
    1 package (3 ounces) lime gelatin
    1 cup boiling water
    1 package (8 ounces) cream cheese

1. Open the can of pineapple. Set a strainer over a medium-size bowl and empty the can of pineapple into the strainer. Set the drained pineapple aside. Measure out ½ cup of pineapple juice that has collected in the bowl and set aside with the pineapple. (Refrigerate the remaining juice for another gelatin dish, or add to orange juice for a refreshing fruit drink.)
2. Put the gelatin, boiling water, and chunks of cream cheese into a blender container. Cover the blender container.
3. Set the blender on high speed and *blend* until the mixture begins to thicken evenly. (If you do not have a blender, place ingredients in a large mixing bowl and use an electric mixer on medium speed.)
4. Pour the gelatin mixture into an 8-inch-square or 9-inch-square pan. Add the reserved crushed pineapple and ½ cup pineapple juice from Step 1. *Stir* with a rubber spatula or large spoon to combine the pineapple evenly with the gelatin mixture. Refrigerate until set.
5. At serving time, *cut* the gelatin salad into squares and serve on individual salad plates.

Broomsticks, Magic Wands, and Satan's Eyes

The ice water helps the broomsticks to open.

> 6 stalks celery
> cold water and ice cubes
> 6 carrots
> 12 to 18 pimiento-stuffed olives

1. Rinse the celery stalks under cold water. On a cutting board, use a paring knife to remove the leaves and end pieces from the celery stalks.
2. *Cut* each stalk in half *crosswise* to yield 12 "broomsticks."
3. Use the paring knife to make 4 or 5 slits (about ⅓ the way up each stalk) on one end only of each of the 12 broomsticks.
4. Partially fill a large bowl with cold water and several ice cubes. Add the broomsticks to the water.
5. *Peel* the carrots with a vegetable peeler.
6. Cut off the ends of the carrots with the paring knife. Then cut each carrot in half crosswise. Carefully divide each carrot half into several sticks or "wands."
7. Add the carrot wands to the ice water with the celery broomsticks. Refrigerate the ice water bowl with the vegetables until serving time.
8. At serving time, *drain* the celery and carrots in a colander. Pat gently with paper towels to remove excess moisture. Arrange the wands and broomsticks on a platter.
9. Add the olives (Satan's Eyes) to the platter and serve.

Hobgoblins' Mud Pie

So sweet that you'll want to serve small portions.

> 1 jar (12 ounces) chocolate fudge sauce
> 9-inch prepared graham cracker pie crust (your own or store bought)
> 1½ pints orange sherbet
> ½ cup (or half of a 6-ounce package) chocolate chips (use mini chocolate chips, if available)

1. Using a rubber spatula, spread the chocolate fudge sauce evenly over the pie crust. Set in the freezer to harden.
2. Remove the sherbet from the freezer to soften.
3. In a medium bowl, combine the sherbet and the chocolate chips with a large spoon.
4. Remove the fudge-bottom crust from the freezer. Carefully spoon on the sherbet–chocolate chip mixture. Smooth the top carefully with a rubber spatula.
5. Return the pie to the freezer until ready to serve.
6. At serving time, remove the pie from the freezer and *cut* into small wedges.

"TRICK OR TREAT" DINNER

Start Phase I about 2 hours and 15 minutes before dinnertime.

Phase	Crossbones Casserole	Green Toad Salad	Broomsticks, Magic Wands, and Satan's Eyes	Hobgoblins' Mud Pie
I				Steps 1–2
II		Steps 1–4		
III			Steps 1–7	
IV				Steps 3–5
V	Steps 1–11			

50-MINUTE BREAKTIME

VI	Step 12			
VII			Steps 8–9	
VIII	Step 13	Step 5		
IX				At dessert time, Step 6

"La Dolce Vita" Dinner

Serves 6

Italian cooking is often regarded as the mother cuisine because it was the first fully developed cuisine in Europe. It was originally inspired by the ancient Romans, who loved good cooking and good eating, and were famous for their sumptuous banquets.

In 1533, Catherine de Médicis brought teams of expert Italian cooks to France, and the secrets of sophisticated Italian cookery spread to Europe and, later, to all of the Western world. Now food lovers in twentieth-century America can relish such treats as pasta, herbed sauces, antipasto, and spumoni.

We have tried to offer you a menu that includes a sampling of *la dolce vita* ("the good life"). We hope you'll enjoy this meal from the first taste of basil-flavored Chicken Appian Way to the last *boccone dolce* ("sweet mouthful") of the tortoni dessert. Dinner will take over one and a half hours from start to finish without a breaktime. You may, however, find a few free moments here and there (for example, while the spaghetti is cooking) to browse through "The Dinner of Trimalchio"—Petronius's meticulous account of what really went on during an ancient Roman feast.

Buon appetito!

Chicken Appian Way
Broken Spaghetti   *Caesar's Salad*
Papa Angelo's Tortoni

Chicken Appian Way

Succulent chicken in a golden sauce with herbs, onions, mushrooms, and zucchini—very much in the Italian tradition.

- 4 pounds frying chicken parts
- 4 tablespoons oil
- 1 tomato
- 1 small onion (or ½ cup frozen chopped onion)
- 1 can Golden Mushroom soup (*not* Cream of Mushroom soup)
- ¼ teaspoon sweet basil
- 1 can (4 ounces) mushroom stems and pieces, undrained
- 2 medium zucchini
  Parmesan cheese

1. Rinse the chicken pieces with cold water. Pat dry with paper towels.
2. Divide the oil between a large skillet and a Dutch oven. Heat the oil over medium-high heat until a drop of water splashed on the oil spatters.
3. Divide the chicken parts between the skillet and the Dutch oven. Brown the chicken on both sides in the hot oil. (You might have to lower the heat if the oil becomes dark and smoky.)
4. While the chicken is browning, prepare the tomato and onion. On a cutting board, using a paring knife, *cut* a ¼-inch deep circle around the stem of the tomato. Remove the stem piece

and discard. *Dice* the tomato. Set the tomato pieces aside until Step 7.

5. Using the paring knife, cut off both ends of the onion and remove the dry outer skin. Finely dice the onion, and set aside until Step 7.

6. When the chicken parts are nicely browned, place all the chicken pieces in the Dutch oven.

7. Add the soup, sweet basil, diced tomato, diced onion, and the can of mushroom stems and pieces (including the liquid) to the chicken in the Dutch oven.

8. Cover the Dutch oven. Reduce the heat to low and *simmer* for 30 minutes.

9. Wash the zucchini under cold water. On a cutting board, using a paring knife, *slice* off both ends of each zucchini. Then cut the zucchini *crosswise* into ¼- to ½-inch slices and add to the chicken. Cover the Dutch oven and continue to simmer for 20 minutes more.

10. Transfer the chicken pieces to a serving dish with tongs or a large spoon. Ladle the sauce over the top of the chicken. Serve with generous sprinkles of Parmesan cheese.

Broken Spaghetti

No Italian meal is complete without some form of pasta.

```
4 to 6  quarts water
     2  tablespoons salt
     2  tablespoons oil
     1  package (16-ounce size) spaghetti
2 to 3  tablespoons butter
```

1. In a large pot, bring the water, salt and oil to a *rapid boil* over a high heat.

2. Break the spaghetti into thirds, and drop carefully into the boiling water. (If the water begins to boil over, reduce the heat, but always maintain a boil.)

3. *Stir* the spaghetti frequently with a spoon to prevent sticking.

Colander

(If your pot is Teflon, use a wooden spoon.) Cook 8 to 12 minutes, or until spaghetti is *al dente*.

4. *Drain* the spaghetti in a colander.
5. Transfer the spaghetti to a large serving dish. Divide the butter into 2 or 3 pieces and place on top of the spaghetti. Toss gently as the butter melts and serve with the sauce from Chicken Appian Way.

Caesar's Salad

While this is not the authentic Caesar salad, it is simple and delicious and fit for a Roman Emperor!

  1 medium head iceberg lettuce
12 black olives, pitted
  2 medium carrots
     salt and pepper
     Italian salad dressing (homemade or store bought)

1. Turn the lettuce head core side up. On a cutting board, using a paring knife, *cut* around the core about 1 inch into the lettuce. Remove the core.
2. Remove any bruised or wilted outer leaves from the lettuce.
3. Rinse the lettuce head under cold water. Allow the lettuce to *drain* for a few moments, core side down, in a colander. Pat off excess moisture with paper towels.
4. Tear off bite-size pieces of lettuce and place in a salad bowl. Add the black olives to the lettuce pieces.
5. On a cutting board, using a paring knife, cut off both ends from the carrots. With a vegetable peeler, remove and discard the outer skin from the carrots.
6. Holding the vegetable peeler directly over the lettuce, scrape the carrots *lengthwise*, letting the strips fall into the salad bowl.

7. Cover the salad with plastic wrap and refrigerate.
8. At serving time, remove the salad from the refrigerator and discard the plastic wrap. *Season* the salad with salt and pepper. Then pour on just enough salad dressing to moisten the lettuce. Toss gently to coat the lettuce pieces evenly.

Papa Angelo's Tortoni

The basic tortoni ingredient can be frozen whipped cream or vanilla ice cream. We use ice cream here because we love the taste and simplicity of Papa's recipe.

1½ pints vanilla ice cream
     dry macaroons or macaroon-type cookies (enough to yield ½ cup crumbs)
18   red and/or green maraschino cherries
¼   teaspoon almond extract

1. Remove the ice cream from the freezer to soften while you proceed with Steps 2 and 3.
2. Using your hands, break up the macaroons, a couple at a time, into a blender container. *Blend* on medium setting until you have ½ cup macaroon crumbs. Set aside 2 tablespoons of the crumbs for Step 7. (If you do not have a blender, put the cookie pieces in a plastic bag and fasten the bag closed. Roll over the bag with a rolling pin to make finer cookie crumbs.)
3. Set aside 6 cherries for a garnish. Then, on a cutting board, using a small, sharp knife, quarter the remaining 12 cherries.
4. In a large bowl, combine the softened ice cream, the macaroon crumbs, the quartered maraschino cherries, and the almond extract.
5. Place 6 paper-cup liners (2½-inch diameter) in a muffin pan.
6. Divide the ice cream mixture evenly among the 6 paper cups.
7. Sprinkle the remaining 2 tablespoons of macaroon crumbs evenly over the ice cream cups. Place the tortoni in the freezer until dessert time.
8. Remove the tortoni from the freezer. Press a whole cherry into the center of each tortoni. Serve on small dessert plates.

"LA DOLCE VITA" DINNER

Begin Phase I about 1 hour and 35 minutes before dinnertime.

Phase	Chicken Appian Way	Broken Spaghetti	Caesar's Salad	Papa Angelo's Tortoni
I	Steps 1–8			
II				Steps 1–7
III			Steps 1–7	
IV	Step 9			
V		Steps 1–5		
VI	Step 10			
VII			Step 8	
VIII				At dessert time, Step 8

"What Have You Got to Lose?" Dinner

Serves 6

Are last year's clothes pinching at the waistline? Are you bulging in your new white slacks? Do you feel embarrassed on the beach in a swimsuit?

If your answer is yes to all three questions, you are among millions of overweight Americans who are concerned about shedding extra pounds. To fight this battle of the bulge, most doctors recommend a regimen of sensible dieting and exercise.

Tonight's dinner is an example of a well-balanced, nutritious, moderate-calorie dinner that is great-tasting. Each recipe serves six people generously, and there'll probably be leftover roast beef for tomorrow. With a four-ounce portion of meat, the entire meal totals about 580 calories per person, including dessert. The titles describe the recipes nicely: Slim 'n' Trim Roast Beef with Oven-Roasted Potatoes, Pounds A-Weigh Vegetable Delight, and Bikini-Beautiful Grapefruit Broil. Plan on starting dinner one hour and forty-five minutes before eating, though less than half that time will be spent in the kitchen. You can use your two long breaktimes for exercising, writing a food plan, and drawing up a progress chart.

You'll have nothing to lose but extra pounds with menus like this one, so if you want to get back into last year's clothes, cut a smooth form in white pants, and look smashing in a swimsuit, serve What Have You Got to Lose? Dinner tonight—and often!

Slim 'n' Trim Roast Beef with Oven-Roasted Potatoes
Pounds A-Weigh Vegetable Delight
Bikini-Beautiful Grapefruit Broil

Slim 'n' Trim Roast Beef with Oven-Roasted Potatoes

This recipe is for roast beef cooked to *medium* doneness (160 degrees on your meat thermometer). Adjust the length of cooking time if you prefer your roast beef rare or well done.

1½ cups water
2½-pound (approx.) sirloin tip roast
  1 medium or 2 small clove(s) fresh garlic
  1 beef bouillon cube
 ½ teaspoon salt
 ⅛ teaspoon pepper
  6 small-to-medium potatoes
 ½ cup water

1. Preheat the oven to 325°F.
2. Place the 1½ cups water in a kettle or saucepan. Bring to a *rapid boil* over high heat.
3. While the water is heating, place the roast, fat side up, in a 13-by-9-inch baking pan.
4. On a cutting board, use a paring knife to *cut* off the tips of the garlic clove(s). Remove the dry outer skin from the garlic, and discard the tips and the skin. Cut the garlic clove(s) to obtain 6 to 8 small pieces of garlic.
5. Use the tip of the paring knife to cut 6 to 8 small slits, about an inch deep, in various places on top of the roast. As you cut each slit, insert a piece of garlic well into that slit.

6. When the water has reached a rapid boil, pour it into a small bowl. *Dissolve* the bouillon cube in the water. (You might want to break up the cube with a fork to speed this process.) Set aside.

7. Combine the salt and pepper in a saucer. Use your hands (which are clean, of course!) to rub the seasonings on the top and sides of the roast.

8. Insert a meat thermometer into the thickest part of the roast. Try to place the thermometer so that its point is in the center of the thickest part of the meat.

9. *Peel* the potatoes with a vegetable peeler. Rinse the potatoes under cold water—then place them in the baking pan around the roast.

10. Pour the bouillon liquid over the roast and potatoes and place in the oven to *bake* for 30 minutes.

11. Using potholders, open the oven door and carefully pull out just a few inches the oven rack with the roast and potatoes on it. *Baste* the roast and potatoes with the pan liquids by spooning the liquid over the food. Be sure to hold the pan securely with potholders in your other hand as you do this. Slide the oven rack back in, close the oven door, and bake for an additional 40 minutes.

12. Using potholders, carefully remove the pan of meat and potatoes from the oven. Check to see if the meat thermometer has reached 160°F. If it has not yet reached 160°F., or if your family prefers meat well done, allow the roast to cook awhile longer until the thermometer reaches 170°F.

13. Use a large fork to transfer only the meat to a serving platter. Let the meat stand at room temperature for about 5 to 10 minutes to seal in the juices and to make carving easier. Meanwhile, add the additional ½ cup of water to the pan with the pan liquids and potatoes and return it to the oven to keep warm. (At this point, you can turn the oven off; there will be enough heat in it to keep the potatoes and pan liquids hot enough until you're ready to eat.)

14. Use a carving knife to *slice* the roast. Then, using potholders, carefully take the baking pan from the oven. With a large spoon, transfer the potatoes to the platter with the roast, and arrange them around the beef slices. Transfer the pan liquids

to a gravy boat or small pitcher. (Note: If some fat rises to the top, use a spoon to skim it off.)

Pounds A-Weigh Vegetable Delight

A colorful and delicious vegetable dish that is easy on the waist-line.

    3 tablespoons vegetable oil
    1 jar (16 ounces) whole onions
    2 packages (10 ounces each) frozen cut green beans
    2 teaspoons sugar
    ¼ teaspoon ground cloves
       salt and pepper to taste
    3 tablespoons water
    1 large bay leaf
    2 medium tomatoes

1. In a large skillet that has a lid, heat the oil over medium heat. (Or use an electric fry pan at 350°F.)
2. *Drain* the onions in a colander or strainer. Place the onions in the skillet; then add the green beans, sugar, cloves, salt, pepper, and water.
3. With your hands, *crumble* the bay leaf into the skillet. Using a large wooden spoon, gently *stir* the vegetables to combine all ingredients.
4. Cover the skillet and continue cooking for about 10 more minutes.
5. While the mixture is cooking, rinse the tomatoes under cold water and place them on a cutting board. With a paring knife, *cut* each tomato into 6 wedges by first cutting it in half through the stem end, then cutting each half into thirds. Be sure to cut off and discard any pieces of dry stem that may be on the wedges.
6. When the onions and green beans have cooked for 10 minutes, remove the lid from the skillet and add the tomato wedges. Cook, uncovered, for an additional 5 minutes.
7. Transfer the vegetables to a serving dish.

Bikini-Beautiful Grapefruit Broil

A new way to enjoy grapefruit! But if strawberries are out of season or too expensive, the grapefruit is delicious all by itself.

  1 pint fresh strawberries
  3 whole grapefruits, white or pink
  2 tablespoons brown sugar

1. Empty the strawberries into a colander. Run cold water over them to clean. *Hull* the berries with your fingers or with a paring knife. Place the berries on a double thickness of paper towels and gently pat dry. Place the prepared berries in a small bowl and refrigerate.
2. On a cutting board, use a large, sharp knife to *cut* each grapefruit in half *crosswise*. Then, with a paring knife, or a special grapefruit knife, cut around the grapefruit between the rind and the fruit. Then cut the grapefruit into sections (along the spokelike membranes) from the center to the rind.
3. Place the 6 prepared grapefruit halves on a baking sheet, cut side up. Distribute the brown sugar evenly over the tops of the 6 grapefruit halves (about 1 teaspoon sugar per grapefruit half). Set the pan of grapefruits aside at room temperature until Step 5.
4. About 25 minutes before dessert time, preheat the oven to 425°F.

Using a grapefruit knife to separate the fruit from the rind.

5. When the oven has reached 425°F., place the baking sheet with the grapefruit halves on the middle rack in the oven and *bake* until the grapefruit is heated and the sugar is melted and bubbly (15 to 20 minutes).
6. Using potholders, carefully remove the baking sheet with the grapefruits from the oven. Set each grapefruit half on an individual dessert plate and set on the dining table. Remove the bowl of berries from the refrigerator, to be spooned over the grapefruit.

"WHAT HAVE YOU GOT TO LOSE?" DINNER

Begin preparations 1 hour and 45 minutes before dinnertime.

Phase	Slim 'n' Trim Roast Beef with Oven-Roasted Potatoes	Pounds A-Weigh Vegetable Delight	Bikini-Beautiful Grapefruits
I	Steps 1–10		
30-MINUTE BREAKTIME			
II	Step 11		
40-MINUTE BREAKTIME			
III			Steps 1–3
IV		Steps 1–4	
V	Steps 12–13		
VI		Steps 5–7	
VII	Step 14		
VIII			25 minutes before dessert time, Steps 4–6

"First Chop" Dinner

Serves 6

The expression *first chop* means "first rate," and in our opinion, this is a first chop menu. Start preparations about one hour and forty-five minutes before you plan to eat dinner. The key to success with this meal is to prepare the pork chops and the scalloped potatoes to go into the oven together for the same amount of cooking time. During the first thirty-five minutes of baking, you will have a substantial breaktime for setting the table, doing your homework, or just plain relaxing. The last thirty-five minutes are scheduled for preparing the green beans and the applesauce. If you follow the chart carefully, the chops, potatoes, and beans should all be ready to serve at the same time.

A final note: Before you leave home in the morning, put the jar of applesauce you'll need for the Spicy Applesauce dessert in the refrigerator to chill.

Betty's Pork Chops
Scalloped Potatoes   Green Beans Amandine
Spicy Applesauce

Betty's Pork Chops

These pork chops are delicious-tasting and special enough to serve to company. To follow this recipe successfully, the chops must be medium thick. If, however, you wish to prepare extra-thick pork chops, be sure to increase the baking time for Step 8 to 1 hour.

> 6 medium-thick pork chops
>   salt and pepper
> 1 medium onion
> 1 medium lemon
> 6 tablespoons brown sugar
> 6 tablespoons chili sauce

1. Preheat the oven to 350°F.
2. *Season* the chops lightly on both sides with salt and pepper.
3. Arrange the chops in a baking dish that has sides at least 1½ inches high.
4. Using a sharp knife, *peel* off and discard the dry outer skin from the onion. *Cut* off both ends of the onion and discard. Cut the onion *crosswise* into 6 slices.
5. Using a sharp knife, cut off both ends of the lemon and discard. Cut the lemon crosswise into 6 slices.
6. On each pork chop, place the following ingredients in the order listed:

> 1 onion slice
> 1 lemon slice
> 1 tablespoon brown sugar
> 1 tablespoon chili sauce

7. Cover the baking dish securely with heavy-duty aluminum foil. Make sure that the foil cover does not touch the ingredients on top of the chops.
8. *Bake* with the foil cover for 35 minutes.
9. Remove the foil and return the chops to the oven uncovered for 35 minutes more.
10. Using a spatula or large fork, lift the chops onto a large serving platter.

Scalloped Potatoes

For extra-special flavor, add 2 tablespoons of fresh, frozen, or dried chopped chives after Step 9.

1 tablespoon butter or margarine
6 medium-size white potatoes
1 small onion
2 tablespoons flour
1 teaspoon salt
  pepper
2 cups milk
  paprika
2 tablespoons butter or margarine

1. Preheat the oven to 350°F.
2. *Grease* a 2-quart casserole with the 1 tablespoon of butter or margarine.
3. *Peel* the potatoes. Using a sharp knife, *slice* the potatoes very thin.
4. Using a sharp knife, remove and discard the dry outer skin from the onion. *Cut* off both ends of the onion and discard. Thinly slice the onion *crosswise,* and separate into rings.
5. Spread half the potato slices on the bottom of the casserole.
6. Sprinkle the flour, ½ teaspoon salt, and a *dash* of pepper over the potatoes.
7. Add all the onion rings in an even layer.

Slicing the onion for rings.

8. Cover the onion rings with the remaining potato slices.
9. Pour the milk over the layers of potato and onion.
10. Sprinkle the top of the casserole with the remaining ½ teaspoon salt and another dash of pepper. Add some generous shakes of paprika.
11. Cut the 2 tablespoons butter or margarine into bits. *Dot* the potatoes.
12. Cover the casserole dish with a lid or aluminum foil.
13. *Bake* for 35 minutes.
14. Remove the cover or foil and return the casserole to the oven to bake for 35 minutes more, or until the potatoes are *fork-tender*.
15. Using potholders, remove the casserole from the oven and set it on a trivet or warming pad.

Green Beans Amandine

Two 10-ounce packages of frozen French-cut green beans can be substituted for the fresh green beans, but the taste just won't be the same. If you do use the frozen beans, however, follow the package instructions for cooking. Then continue with Step 4 below.

       1½ pounds fresh green beans
            boiling water (in a kettle or medium-size saucepan)
        1 teaspoon salt
   2 to 3 tablespoons butter or margarine
       ⅓ cup sliced almonds
            salt to taste

1. Rinse the beans under cold water. Using your fingers, snap off and discard the ends of the beans.
2. Place the beans and 1 teaspoon salt in a large saucepan. Add just enough boiling water from the kettle to cover the beans.
3. Cover the saucepan and *simmer* the beans over medium heat for about 15 minutes (if you like your beans crisp, as we do).
4. While the beans are simmering, *melt* the butter or margarine in a small saucepan over low heat.

5. Add the almonds to the melted butter and toss gently to coat. Be careful not to brown the butter.
6. Cook the almonds in the butter over low heat until they are brown and toasty.
7. When the beans are done, *drain* them in a colander to remove all the water.
8. Place the drained beans in a serving dish. Pour over the almond-butter mixture and *foss* gently to combine.

Spicy Applesauce

Try to chill the applesauce early in the day. If you have homemade applesauce on hand, this dessert will be even better.

   1 jar (32 ounces) applesauce
   whipped topping (optional)
   nutmeg and/or cinnamon, to taste

1. Spoon a generous helping of applesauce into each of 6 individual dessert bowls. Place the dishes in the refrigerator to keep cold.
2. Top each serving with a *dollop* of whipped topping, if desired.
3. Sprinkle with nutmeg and/or cinnamon, to taste.

"FIRST CHOP" DINNER

Begin Phase I about 1 hour and 45 minutes before dinnertime.

Phase	Betty's Pork Chops	Scalloped Potatoes	Green Beans Amandine	Spicy Applesauce
I		Steps 1–12		
II	Steps 2–7			
III	Step 8	Step 13		

35-MINUTE BREAKTIME

Phase	Betty's Pork Chops	Scalloped Potatoes	Green Beans Amandine	Spicy Applesauce
IV	Step 9	Step 14		
V			Steps 1–6	
VI				Step 1
VII			Steps 7–8	
VIII	Step 10	Step 15		
IX				At dessert time, Steps 2–3

"Sweetheart" Dinner

Serves 6

Legends vary as to how we came to celebrate St. Valentine's Day. Many years ago, the English believed that birds chose their mates on February 14 because they knew that spring was near. Young people, following the example of the birds, chose their sweethearts on that same date.

The Romans used to celebrate Lupercalia on February 15. On that day, the young girls would put their names in a box, and each young man would draw out the name of his next year's sweetheart. The young couples would often send sweet messages and gifts to each other. Years later, the Christians changed the date to February 14 and designated the holiday in honor of two Roman heroes named Valentine.

Today, these messages are usually sent by mail and called valentines. To celebrate the occasion at your house, we have prepared a menu that is very red and pink. You need to set aside about one and a half hours from the time you begin until dinner. If you work efficiently, you might have up to a fifteen-minute breaktime—just long enough to add a few words of sentiment to a valentine for someone special.

Heart-y Salmon Loaf with Pink Sauce
Let-Us Have Peas   Cupid's Waldorf Salad
Queen of Hearts' Strawberry Tarts

Heart-y Salmon Loaf With Pink Sauce

HEART-Y SALMON LOAF

Pink and pretty for Valentine's Day!

    1 can (about 15½ ounces) salmon
    2 eggs
    1 cup bread crumbs (soft or dry)
    1 cup milk
    2 stalks celery
       pepper
    1 teaspoon celery salt
    1 teaspoon onion salt
    2 tablespoons butter or margarine

1. Preheat the oven to 350°F.
2. *Drain* the liquid from the can of salmon into a small saucer. Set the liquid aside to use in the Pink Sauce.
3. Empty the salmon into a large bowl. Remove any skin and bones.
4. Break the eggs into a small bowl. *Beat* with a wire whisk or fork and pour into the bowl with the salmon.
5. Add the bread crumbs and milk to the salmon-egg mixture. *Stir* to combine ingredients.
6. On a cutting board, using a paring knife, *cut* off the leaves and ends from the celery stalks. Discard the ends. (Save the leaves in a plastic bag in the refrigerator to add to soups or green salads.) Rinse the stalks under cold water. Shake off any excess water.
7. Using the paring knife, finely *dice* the celery stalks.
8. Add the diced celery, a *dash* of pepper, and the celery salt and onion salt to the salmon mixture. Stir until the ingredients are well blended.

9. Turn the salmon mixture into a loaf pan, about 9 inches by 5 inches by 3 inches. Pat the mixture down with the back of a spoon. *Dot* with the butter.
10. Cover the loaf pan tightly with aluminum foil.
11. *Bake* for 30 minutes.
12. Remove the foil cover and bake for 30 minutes longer.
13. Using potholders, remove the pan from the oven. *Slice* the salmon loaf *crosswise* into 6 portions.
14. Serve with Pink Sauce.

PINK SAUCE

Elegant over Heart-y Salmon Loaf!

    1 tablespoon butter
      reserved salmon liquid (from the Heart-y Salmon Loaf recipe)
    ½ cup milk
    1 tablespoon flour
    ½ cup ketchup
      salt and pepper

1. *Melt* the butter in a medium saucepan over medium-low heat.
2. Add the salmon liquid and ¼ cup milk. Bring just to a *boil*.
3. While the above mixture is reaching a boil, *blend* together in a small bowl the flour and the additional ¼ cup milk.
4. When the salmon liquid-butter-milk mixture reaches a boil, slowly pour in the flour-milk mixture, *stirring* constantly with a wooden spoon. Reduce the heat to low and continue to stir for 2 to 3 minutes.
5. Add the ketchup. Then taste the sauce and *season* with salt and pepper to taste.
6. Transfer the Pink Sauce to a small bowl or gravy boat, to spoon over the Heart-y Salmon Loaf.

Let-Us Have Peas

The French use lettuce to provide the moisture for cooking peas. This process also combines the subtle flavors of the two vegetables.

When we tried out this menu, one of our husbands couldn't imagine our putting lettuce leaves in with the peas. Later, he exclaimed: "These are the best peas I've ever eaten!"

4 to 6 large, outside lettuce leaves (from an iceberg lettuce)
    1 tablespoon butter or margarine
    2 packages (10 ounces each, or one 20-ounce bag) frozen peas
   ¼ teaspoon sugar
   ½ teaspoon salt
   ⅛ teaspoon pepper
    3 tablespoons butter

1. Rinse the lettuce leaves under cold water. Gently pat dry with paper towels.
2. In a large skillet with a tight-fitting lid (or an electric fry pan), *melt* the 1 tablespoon butter over medium heat (if using an electric fry pan, set the dial at 340°F.).
3. Cover the bottom of the skillet containing the melted butter with 2 or 3 lettuce leaves.
4. Place the frozen peas on the lettuce leaves.
5. Sprinkle the peas evenly with the sugar, salt, and pepper.
6. *Dot* the peas with the 3 tablespoons butter.
7. Cover the peas with the remaining 2 or 3 lettuce leaves.
8. Cover the skillet and *simmer* over low heat for 20 minutes. (If using an electric fry pan, the dial probably has a simmer setting.)
9. At serving time, discard all the lettuce leaves and transfer the peas and their liquid to a serving dish.

Lettuce leaves provide moisture for cooking peas French-style.

Cupid's Waldorf Salad

The bright red skins of the apples make this salad ideal for a Valentine's Day dinner.

   3 medium, bright red eating apples
  3 to 4 stalks celery
    1 lemon wedge (optional)
    ½ cup (2½-ounce package) chopped walnuts
    ½ cup mayonnaise

1. Rinse the apples and celery stalks and pat dry with paper towels.
2. On a cutting board, using a paring knife, *cut* each apple into 8 slices. Remove the core parts. Then cut each slice into thirds. Place the apple pieces in a medium serving bowl. Squeeze the juice from the lemon wedge over the apple pieces to prevent browning.
3. On the cutting board, use the paring knife to cut off the leaves and ends of the celery stalks. Discard the ends. (Save the leaves in a plastic bag in the refrigerator to use in soup or green salad.) *Slice* the celery stalks and place the celery slices in the bowl with the apple pieces.
4. Add the chopped walnuts to the apples and celery.
5. Add the mayonnaise, and *mix* gently to combine all ingredients.
6. Cover the Waldorf Salad with plastic wrap and place in the refrigerator until serving time.
7. Remove the salad from the refrigerator, discard the plastic wrap, and serve.

Queen of Hearts' Strawberry Tarts

If you prefer to make the Queen's Pie, follow the same directions given below for the tarts—just substitute a 9-inch graham cracker piecrust (your own or store-bought) for the tart shells and increase the ice cream to 1½ pints and the jam to ½ cup.

1 pint strawberry ice cream
1 package (4 ounces) graham cracker tart shells—6 shells to a package (or make your own tart shells)
⅓ cup strawberry jam
1 cup (from about a 7½-ounce jar) marshmallow fluff, topping, or creme
cinnamon heart candies, red sugar, sprinkles, or other red decorative candies

1. Remove the ice cream from the freezer and allow it to soften slightly.
2. Divide the jam equally among the 6 tart shells.
3. Spoon the softened ice cream among the 6 tart shells, covering the jam. Place the tarts in the freezer for about 20 minutes, in order for the ice cream to harden.
4. Spoon the marshmallow topping over the 6 tarts. Then dip a rubber spatula in hot water to spread the topping evenly over the ice cream.
5. Decorate the tops of the tarts with the candies, making your own designs or love symbols.
6. Return the tarts to the freezer until dessert time.
7. Carefully remove the foil pans from the tarts. Place each tart on a small plate (use paper doilies if you have them) and serve with a kiss.

"SWEETHEART" DINNER

Start Phase I about 1½ hours before dinnertime.

Phase	Heart-y Salmon Loaf	Pink Sauce	Let-Us Have Peas	Cupid's Waldorf Salad	Queen of Hearts' Strawberry Tarts
I					Steps 1–3
II	Steps 1–11				
III					Steps 4–6
IV				Steps 1–6	
V	Step 12				
VI			Steps 1–8		

POSSIBLE BRIEF BREAKTIME

Phase	Heart-y Salmon Loaf	Pink Sauce	Let-Us Have Peas	Cupid's Waldorf Salad	Queen of Hearts' Strawberry Tarts
VII		Steps 1–6			
VIII	Steps 13–14		Step 9	Step 7	
IX					At dessert time, Step 7

"Chilly Night" Dinner

Serves 6

What makes chili taste like chili? Chili gets its characteristic taste
from the fiery vegetable chili, a cousin to the green bell pepper.
Over 140 varieties are grown in Mexico. The chipotle and mulato
peppers, in particular, have been regarded in certain areas with
almost mystical reverence. These two peppers have become the
national seasoning of Mexico and are the sources for the chili
powder that most Americans use in their chili recipes today.

Chili has become so popular in the United States that an an-
nual chili-making contest in Texas attracts people from all over
the country. Entries include hot chili, chili with dollops of sour
cream, chili with a touch of lime—you name it!

Our Chilly Night Chili may not be fancy, but it is easy to prepare, economical, and, above all, delicious. It's great served in
ceramic bowls with squares of Kathy's homemade Corn Bread,
and with Summer's Coming Fruit Plate on the side. Dessert is
cold, refreshing Dreamsicle Scoops, a perfect counter for the hot,
spicy taste of chili. Dinner must be started one hour and twenty
minutes before eating, but plan on a forty-minute breaktime away
from the kitchen.

When winter winds start to blow, and when the temperature

dips way down, you can warm the hearts of family and friends with Chilly Night Dinner.

Chilly Night Chili
Summer's Coming Fruit Plate   *Kathy's Corn Bread*
Dreamsicle Scoops

Chilly Night Chili

For thicker chili, drain off the liquid from one of the two cans of tomatoes in Step 5.

   2 cups frozen chopped onion, or 2 medium onions
   2 small green peppers
   2 pounds ground chuck or extra-lean ground beef
   2 cans (16 ounces each) tomatoes
   2 cans (16 ounces each) dark red kidney beans
   1 can (15 to 16 ounces) tomato sauce
   2 teaspoons salt
   1 tablespoon chili powder
   2 bay leaves (optional)

1. If using fresh onions: with a paring knife, *cut* off and discard both ends of each onion. Discard the ends. *Peel* off the dry outer skins. *Chop* the onion on a cutting board. Set aside.
2. Rinse the green peppers under cold water. Shake to remove any excess moisture. With the paring knife, remove the stems from the peppers by cutting a circle around each stem end and lifting the stem out. Cut the peppers in half. Remove and discard the seeds. On the cutting board, cut the peppers into *lengthwise* strips, about 1/8-inch wide. Then cut the strips *crosswise* to obtain small pieces of pepper. Set aside.
3. Heat a Dutch oven over medium-high heat until a drop of water splashed on the surface spatters. Add the ground beef, the fresh or frozen chopped onion, and the green pepper pieces. *Stir* with a wooden spoon to break up the meat and to combine the ingredients. Cook until the meat is browned and the vegetables are tender, about 10 minutes.

4. Using a large metal spoon, spoon off as much excess fat from the meat-vegetable mixture as possible.
5. Add the tomatoes with their liquid. Stir with a spoon to break up the tomatoes.
6. Add the kidney beans with their liquid to the ingredients in the Dutch oven, along with the tomato sauce, salt, chili powder, and bay leaves.
7. Cover the Dutch oven and *simmer* gently over low to medium heat for 1¼ hours.
8. At serving time, remove the bay leaves from the chili. Spoon the chili into individual soup bowls or serve from a large tureen at the table.

Summer's Coming Fruit Plate

Fruit and cheese also make a great dessert combination. If you ever want to make this recipe several hours in advance, be sure to dip the cut apples and pears in orange or lemon juice to prevent browning.

6 large lettuce leaves (from iceberg lettuce)
4 medium-to-large apples or pears, or 2 apples and 2 pears
   chunk of Cheddar, Colby, or brick cheese (4 to 6 ounces)

1. Rinse the lettuce leaves under cold water. Gently pat dry with paper towels. Place a leaf on each of 6 small salad plates.
2. Rinse the fruit under cold water. Pat dry with paper towels. On a cutting board, use a sharp knife to *cut* each apple or pear in half. Then *slice* each apple or pear half into thirds. Cut out and discard the core part from each fruit slice.
3. Divide the fruit wedges evenly among the 6 salad plates, alternating apples and pears, if using both fruits.
4. Cut the cheese *crosswise* into 12 pieces. Place 2 cheese slices on top of each fruit plate.

Fruit and cheese arranged attractively on lettuce leaf.

Kathy's Corn Bread

Kathy likes to put soft butter and marmalade on her corn bread.

 1 tablespoon shortening, butter, or margarine
⅓ cup butter or margarine
1⅔ cups flour
⅔ cup sugar
 1 tablespoon plus 2 teaspoons baking powder
 1 teaspoon salt
1⅔ cups yellow cornmeal
 2 eggs
1⅔ cups milk

1. Preheat the oven to 425°F.
2. *Grease* a 9-inch-square pan with the 1 tablespoon of shortening, butter, or margarine.
3. In a small saucepan over low heat, *melt* the ⅓ cup butter or margarine.
4. While the butter is melting, place the flour, sugar, baking powder, salt, and cornmeal in a large mixing bowl. With a large spoon, *stir* the dry ingredients until blended.
5. Break the eggs into a small bowl. *Beat* the eggs with a wire whisk or fork. Add the beaten eggs, along with the milk, to the dry ingredients in the large mixing bowl. Stir gently, just until the dry ingredients are moistened.
6. Add the melted butter to the batter and stir just until blended. Do not overstir!
7. Using a rubber spatula, transfer the cornmeal batter to the greased pan. Smooth the top of the mixture with the spatula.
8. *Bake* on the middle rack of the oven for 40 minutes, or until the corn bread is golden and a toothpick inserted near the center comes out clean.
9. Using potholders, carefully remove the corn bread from the oven and cool in the pan (on a wire rack, if you have one) for about 10 minutes.
10. *Cut* the corn bread into squares. Place the squares in a napkin-lined breadbasket.

Dreamsicle Scoops

The combination of vanilla ice cream and orange sherbet is a "dream come true" and the perfect finale to a chili dinner.

1 quart vanilla ice cream
1 pint orange sherbet

1. Using an ice cream scoop or server, scoop 1 large scoop of ice cream and 1 small scoop of sherbet into 6 dessert bowls.

"CHILLY NIGHT" DINNER

Begin preparations about 1 hour and 20 minutes before dinnertime.

Phase	Chilly Night Chili	Summer's Coming Fruit Plate	Kathy's Corn Bread	Dreamsicle Scoops
I	Steps 1–7			
II			Steps 1–8	
40-MINUTE BREAKTIME				
III			Step 9	
IV		Steps 1–4		
V			Step 10	
VI	Step 8			
VII				At dessert time, Step 1

"What's in a Name?" Dinner

Serves 6

What's in a name? that which we call a rose
By any other name would smell as sweet.
William Shakespeare
(*Romeo and Juliet*, II, ii)

A name may be just a label, but wouldn't it be neat to have a recipe named after you? Tonight's meatless menu features recipes that bear people's names. Start preparing about one hour and forty minutes before dinner, but count on a fifteen-minute breaktime to check out the following information:

QUICHE LORRAINE

Lorraine, the French province near Germany (and also a girl's name), is considered to be the birthplace of quiche (pronounced *keesh*). Many believe that the word *quiche* is a derivative of the German word *kuchen,* meaning cake. The classic Quiche Lorraine blends together eggs, cream, bacon, and Swiss or Gruyère cheese.

In Alsace, a neighboring province of Lorraine, onions are added, just as in our recipe. Our quiche might therefore be called Quiche Alsace, but, as Shakespeare suggests, by any name it will taste delicious.

BASIL'S MUSHROOMS

Our friend Basil concocted this recipe, using the powerful herb of his namesake. Basil, or *Ocimum basilicum,* is a member of the mint family, and is used to enhance the flavor of Italian sauces, salads, and dressings, meat, fish and egg dishes, and fresh vegetables. The basil in tonight's menu adds a distinctive taste to mushrooms, creating a wonderful topping for our quiche.

CAESAR 3-BEAN SALAD

A visiting cousin claims that the Caesar in Caesar salad refers to Caesar Cabrini of Acapulco. Caesar Cabrini evidently made the first Caesar salad, using whole leaves of romaine lettuce, a coddled egg, garlic, Parmesan cheese, oil and vinegar, and croutons. Our Caesar 3-Bean Salad is a variation, featuring beans instead of lettuce.

PEACH MELBA

Peach Melba is a popular dessert on at least two continents, Australia and North America. It takes its name from Nellie Melba, beloved Australian operatic soprano.

Want to make a name for yourself? Serve this easy-to-prepare, meatless, gourmet-style dinner to your family and friends tonight.

Quiche Lorraine with Basil's Mushrooms
Caesar 3-Bean Salad
Peach Melba

Quiche Lorraine

Quiche is great luncheon fare too. It can be prepared earlier in the day, refrigerated, and then baked just before serving time.

    2 9-inch piecrusts, unbaked (your own, or store-bought frozen shells)
    2 medium onions
    6 tablespoons butter (¾ stick)
    1 block (12 to 14 ounces) Swiss cheese
    6 medium-to-large eggs
    1 pint (2 cups) half-and-half
    1 cup milk
    2 teaspoons salt
    ½ teaspoon pepper
       dash of nutmeg (or more, if desired)

1. Preheat the oven to 450°F.
2. Prick the bottoms and sides of the two piecrusts in several places with the tines of a fork. (This will prevent the crusts from puffing up.)
3. While the oven is heating, set the onions on a cutting board. Use a paring knife to *cut* off both ends of the onions. Remove the dry outer skins from the onions. Discard the ends and the outer skins. Then use a sharp knife to *chop* the onions.
4. In a large skillet over medium heat, *melt* the butter. When the butter is melted, add the chopped onions and *sauté* until soft, *stirring* from time to time with a fork to cook evenly, about 12 minutes. (Use a wooden spoon if your skillet is Teflon.)
5. While the onions are cooking, place the piecrusts on the center rack in the preheated oven and *bake* for 5 minutes. (This prevents a soggy crust.) After 5 minutes, remove the crusts carefully from the oven, using potholders. Do not turn the oven temperature down or off.
6. When the onions are soft and golden, divide them evenly between the two partially baked piecrusts. Spread the onions with a rubber spatula. Set aside until Step 8.

Grating the cheese for the quiche.

7. Place the grater in a large mixing bowl. *Grate* the entire block of Swiss cheese. Sprinkle half the grated cheese over the onions in each pie shell.

8. Break the eggs into the bowl that you just used for grating the cheese. Add the half-and-half, milk, salt, pepper, and nutmeg. Hold the bowl at a slight tilt and with a wire whisk or fork in your other hand, *beat* the egg mixture until it is well blended with the other ingredients. Pour this mixture over the onions and cheese in the two pie shells.

9. Place both pies on the center rack of the oven. Bake for 15 minutes.

10. After the quiches have baked at 450°F. for 15 minutes, lower the oven temperature to 350°F. and bake for 15 to 20 minutes longer.

11. When the quiches have finished baking, use potholders to pull the oven rack out halfway. Insert the blade of a table knife into one of the pies. If the blade comes out clean, the quiches are done. If not, bake at 350°F. for 5 minutes longer, or until they test done.

12. When the quiches are done, use potholders to remove them from the oven. Place the quiches on a wire rack and let stand for 5 minutes to set.

Wire Whisk

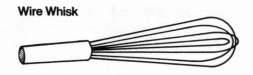

13. With a large knife, cut each quiche into 6 wedges. Use a spatula to lift two quiche wedges onto each dinner plate.
14. Pass Basil's Mushrooms to be spooned generously over the quiche wedges.

Basil's Mushrooms

The basil adds a nice flavor.

   1 pound fresh mushrooms
   3 tablespoons butter
  ½ teaspoon salt
   1 teaspoon dry basil

1. Place the mushrooms in a colander and rinse thoroughly with cold water. Gently shake the colander to remove any excess water. Pat the mushrooms dry with paper towels.
2. Place the mushrooms on a cutting board. Use a paring knife to *cut* off about ¼ inch from the tough end portion of each mushroom stem. Then *slice* the mushrooms in thirds *lengthwise*, cutting through both the cap and the stem.
3. *Melt* the butter in a large skillet over medium-high heat. When the butter is melted, add the sliced mushrooms. Sprinkle with the salt and the basil. *Sauté* the mushrooms, *stirring* every few minutes with a fork until they are tender. Then turn the heat down to the very lowest setting and keep the mushrooms warm in the pan until serving time.
4. Carefully transfer the mushrooms to a small serving bowl to spoon over wedges of Quiche Lorraine.

Caesar 3-Bean Salad

This is a great salad for picnics and potlucks. Steps 1–3 can be prepared a day ahead. Then add the Parmesan cheese and croutons just before serving.

   1 can (8 ounces) cut green beans
   1 can (8 ounces) red kidney beans
   8 ounces (half of a 16-ounce can) garbanzo beans
  ¼ cup Caesar salad dressing (your own or store-bought)
   2 tablespoons grated Parmesan cheese
  ½ cup croutons (optional)

1. *Drain* the green beans, kidney beans, and garbanzo beans in a colander or strainer. Shake gently to remove excess liquid.
2. Place the beans in a shallow pan. (A 9-inch-square baking pan will do nicely.) Pour the Caesar salad dressing over the beans. Toss gently with a large spoon to coat all the beans with the dressing.
3. Cover the bean mixture with plastic wrap and refrigerate until serving time.
4. At serving time, remove and discard the plastic wrap. Transfer the beans to a medium-size serving bowl.
5. Sprinkle Parmesan cheese over the beans. Add croutons, if desired.

Peach Melba

The original version features vanilla ice cream, but we like to substitute peach, strawberry, or pistachio.

   6 canned peach halves (from a 29-ounce can)
  ⅓ cup red raspberry jelly (not jam)
 1½ pints ice cream

1. With a slotted spoon, lift the peach halves one at a time from the can. Place a peach half, hollow side up, in each of 6 dessert bowls.
2. *Melt* the raspberry jelly in a small saucepan over low heat. (Watch it carefully, because this will take only a few minutes.)
3. Distribute the melted jelly among the 6 peach halves. Refrigerate until dessert time.
4. At dessert time, top each peach half with a generous scoop of ice cream.

"WHAT'S IN A NAME?" DINNER

Begin preparations about 1 hour and 40 minutes before dinnertime.

Phase	Quiche Lorraine	Basil's Mushrooms	Caesar 3-Bean Salad	Peach Melba
I			Steps 1–3	
II				Steps 1–3
III	Steps 1–9			

15-MINUTE BREAKTIME

Phase	Quiche Lorraine	Basil's Mushrooms	Caesar 3-Bean Salad	Peach Melba
IV	Step 10			
V		Steps 1–3		
VI	Steps 11–12			
VII			Steps 4–5	
VIII		Step 4		
IX	Steps 13–14			
X				At dessert time, Step 4

"Irish Luck" Dinner

Serves 6

Sometime in the fourth century, a man named Patricius was born in Britain. When Patricius was sixteen, Irish raiders kidnapped him from his father's villa and sent him to Ireland as a slave. For six years, Patricius worked in Ireland as a shepherd, until he finally managed to escape and return home to Britain. But Patricius was not content in Britain. He felt a calling to return to Ireland to "convert the heathen." So it was Patricius, later known as St. Patrick, who established Christianity in Ireland.

By the seventh century, St. Patrick had become the national apostle of Ireland and quite a legendary figure. One legend has to do with the shamrock as the national flower of Ireland. It is said that the shamrock is worn by the Irish on St. Patrick's Day because St. Patrick himself had used the three-leaved plant to explain the concept of the Holy Trinity to nonbelievers. Another legend credits St. Patrick with driving snakes out of Ireland and into the sea. To this day, there are no snakes in all of Ireland— in fact, the only reptile there is the newt.

As you know, St. Patrick's Day is celebrated on March 17. In honor of this occasion, we suggest that you serve your family and friends a special Irish Luck menu. You'll have to get right to work on it, though, because it takes three hours from start to finish. Nevertheless, you'll have three long breaktimes that add up to over two hours.

Complement St. Pat's Corned Beef and Cabbage and Lepre-chaun's Ring-o-Gold Fruit Salad with a basket of warm clover-leaf rolls, and you'll have a dinner that's as Irish as Mulligan stew. We'd like to claim that the Shamrock Ice Cream Pie dessert is too, but that would be more than a wee bit of blarney!

St. Pat's Corned Beef and Cabbage
Leprechaun's Ring-o-Gold Fruit Salad
Shamrock Ice Cream Pie

St. Pat's Corned Beef and Cabbage

This hearty dish includes potatoes, another popular Irish food.

   3 to 3½ pounds lean corned beef brisket
              water
         6 medium potatoes
         6 small onions
         6 medium carrots
         1 medium green cabbage

1. Place the brisket in a Dutch oven or a 5- to 6-quart casserole that has a lid. Add hot water to the Dutch oven until the water level is about 1 inch higher than the top of the meat.
2. Bring the water with the meat in it to a *rapid boil* over high heat. With a spoon, skim off and discard any fat or scum that rises to the surface.
3. Cover the Dutch oven or casserole. Lower the heat but main-tain a *simmer*. Simmer the meat, covered, for 2¼ hours.
4. Use a vegetable peeler to *peel* the potatoes. Place the pared potatoes on a cutting board and use a sharp knife to *cut* the potatoes in half. Using potholders, carefully remove the lid from the Dutch oven and place the potatoes in with the meat. Do not cover the Dutch oven.

5. Place the onions on the cutting board. Use a paring knife to cut off the ends of the onions. Discard the ends. Peel off and discard the dry outer skins. Add the onions to the Dutch oven but do not cover.

6. Place the carrots on the cutting board. Use the paring knife to cut off both ends of the carrots. Discard the ends. Use a vegetable peeler to peel the carrots *lengthwise*. Place the peeled carrots in the Dutch oven with the meat, potatoes, and onions.

7. Increase the heat just enough to return the liquid in the Dutch oven to a simmer. Cover the Dutch oven and simmer for 20 minutes more.

8. Discard any bruised or wilted outer leaves of the cabbage. Rinse the cabbage under cold water, core side down. With a large, sharp cutting knife, cut the cabbage in half through the stem end. Cut each cabbage half into thirds to obtain 6 wedges. Using potholders, carefully remove the lid from the Dutch oven and add the cabbage wedges to the corned beef and vegetables.

9. When the liquid has returned to a simmer, cover the Dutch oven again. Continue to simmer for another 10 to 15 minutes, or until the meat and vegetables are *fork-tender*.

10. Using a large fork, carefully transfer the corned beef to the cutting board. Use a sharp knife to cut several *crosswise* slices of meat (see picture for how to cut meat across the grain). Set the large, unsliced piece of meat, along with the slices of meat, on a large serving platter.

11. With a slotted spoon, remove the vegetables from the Dutch oven and set them attractively on the large platter around the meat.

Slicing the corned beef.

Leprechaun's Ring-o-Gold Fruit Salad

A treasure of a salad!

    6 large lettuce leaves (outer leaves from a head of an
      iceberg lettuce)
    1 can (20 ounces) pineapple rings, chilled
    1 can (16 ounces) whole-berry cranberry sauce
    ⅓ cup chopped nuts (optional)

1. Wash the lettuce leaves under cold water. Gently pat dry with
   paper towels. Place a lettuce leaf on each of 6 salad plates.
2. Using a fork, carefully lift out the pineapple rings from the
   can. Set 1 pineapple ring on each lettuce leaf. (Refrigerate
   the remaining pineapple with its syrup, to be enjoyed at another time—as a healthy snack, part of a fruit salad, or in a
   gelatin dish.)
3. Place 1 heaping tablespoon of the cranberry sauce in the
   center of each pineapple ring. (Store the remaining cranberry
   sauce in the refrigerator.)
4. Sprinkle the pineapple-cranberry salads with chopped nuts,
   if desired. (If you make this salad well in advance of eating
   it, cover the salad plates with plastic wrap to prevent drying
   of the pineapple and cranberry sauce.) Refrigerate the salads
   until serving time.
5. At serving time, take the salad plates from the refrigerator and
   serve.

Shamrock Ice Cream Pie

All Irish eyes will be smiling when you bring out this dessert treat.

    1 quart vanilla ice cream
    1 pint lime sherbet
    1 9-inch graham cracker piecrust (homemade or store-bought)
      green gumdrops (optional)

1. Remove the ice cream and sherbet from the freezer and allow
   to soften slightly.

2. Spoon the vanilla ice cream over the bottom of the piecrust, smoothing evenly with a rubber spatula.
3. Gently spoon the lime sherbet over the vanilla ice cream, smoothing the sherbet evenly with the rubber spatula.
4. Cover the pie with plastic wrap and return the pie to the freezer until serving time.
5. At serving time, remove the pie from the freezer and discard the plastic wrap. If you wish, decorate the top of the pie with halves of green gumdrops arranged in the shape of shamrocks. With a sharp knife, *cut* the pie into wedges and place on individual dessert plates. (If you have difficulty slicing the pie, let it stand at room temperature for a few minutes before slicing.)

"IRISH LUCK" DINNER

Begin preparations 3 hours before dinnertime.

Phase	St. Pat's Corned Beef and Cabbage	Leprechaun's Ring-o-Gold Fruit Salad	Shamrock Ice Cream Pie
I	Steps 1–3		
II			Step 1
III		Steps 1–4	
IV			Steps 2–4
70-MINUTE BREAKTIME			
V	Steps 4–7		
15–MINUTE BREAKTIME			
VI	Steps 8–9		
10–15-MINUTE BREAKTIME			
VII		Step 5	
VIII	Steps 10–11		
IX			At dessert time, Step 5

"Let's Talk Turkey" Dinner

Serves 6

To "talk turkey," according to the dictionary, is to talk candidly and bluntly. We are talking turkey when we say that tonight's menu is an all-out winner.

The surprise ingredients in the Cold Turkey Salad are pineapple chunks and sliced almonds. Add a sprinkling of dill to fresh tomato slices and, *voilà,* Dilly Tomatoes. How about extending the menu with dinner rolls and butter, a dish of your favorite pickles and olives, and a bowl of crunchy potato chips. On cold days, try adding a heated beverage, such as warmed cranberry juice or apple cider. Then, at dessert time, bring out the rich, chocolaty Mock Dobos Torte for an impressive finale. There isn't a breaktime with this meal, but everything can be prepared and ready to eat in only one hour.

Where do you get the cooked turkey? This is one of the few meals in this book that depends on leftovers. Whenever your family has a turkey dinner, aren't there always leftovers?

Plan to serve Let's Talk Turkey Dinner whenever there's leftover turkey at your house. Your family and friends will gobble it up every time.

Cold Turkey Salad
Dilly Tomatoes
Mock Dobos Torte

Cold Turkey Salad

A fabulous way to use leftover turkey. Or substitute cooked chicken.

enough leftover turkey (or chicken) to equal 4 to 5 cups when cut into large cubes
2 to 3 stalks celery
1 small can (8 ounces) pineapple chunks
¾ teaspoon salt
⅔ cup mayonnaise
½ cup sliced almonds (Carole likes to toast the almonds for her salad)

1. On a cutting board, using a sharp knife, *cut* the turkey meat into large cubes. Discard any pieces of skin, bone, or cartilage. Place the turkey cubes in a large mixing bowl.
2. Rinse the celery stalks under cold water. Pat dry with paper towels. On a cutting board, use a paring knife to remove the leaves and end pieces from the celery stalks. Discard the end pieces. (Save the leaves in a plastic bag in the refrigerator to add to soup or green salads.)
3. Cut the celery stalks *on the diagonal* into ⅓-inch slices. Add the sliced celery to the turkey pieces.
4. *Drain* the pineapple chunks into a strainer over a bowl. (Save the juice to add to a gelatin dish or drink it as a healthy snack.) On a cutting board, use a sharp knife to halve each pineapple chunk. Add the pineapple pieces to the bowl with the turkey and celery.
5. Sprinkle the salt over the turkey mixture.
6. Add the mayonnaise to the turkey mixture. Use a large spoon to gently combine the ingredients and to coat evenly with the mayonnaise.
7. Transfer the turkey salad to a 1½- or 2-quart serving dish. Sprinkle the top of the salad evenly with the sliced almonds.

8. Cover with plastic wrap and refrigerate until serving time.
9. Remove the plastic wrap from the turkey salad and serve.

Dilly Tomatoes

In colonial America, dill was often hung in doorways to ward off witches, boiled in wine as a hiccup tonic, and grown in kitchen corners for its aroma. Dill seeds were frequently given to children for nibbling during long church services. Today we associate dill mainly with pickles, but its pungent flavor is wonderful with sweet and bland vegetables. We seasoned red, ripe tomato slices with dillweed for this tasty dish.

    4 medium tomatoes
      salt to taste
      dillweed (fresh or dried)

1. Rinse the tomatoes under cold water. Gently pat dry with paper towels.
2. On a cutting board, use a sharp knife to *cut* each tomato *crosswise* into several slices. Cut out and discard the core section.
3. Arrange the tomato slices in a single layer (overlapping slightly) on a serving plate.
4. Lightly *season* the tomatoes with salt. Then sprinkle moderately with dillweed.

Mock Dobos Torte

A true Dobos torte, or *Dobos torta,* as they say in Hungary, is an elegant, many-layered sponge cake filled with chocolate cream and glazed with caramelized sugar. Here we offer a simplified, mock version, substituting prepared pound cake for the sponge cake, and alternating layers of chocolate frosting with apricot jam.

CHOCOLATE CREAM CHEESE FROSTING (*for the torte*)

¼ cup (½ stick) butter or margarine
1 package (3 ounces) cream cheese
2 squares (1 ounce each) unsweetened chocolate
2½ cups powdered (confectioners') sugar
2 tablespoons milk (more, if needed)

1. Remove the butter and cream cheese from the refrigerator. Let stand at room temperature to soften.
2. *Melt* the chocolate in a double boiler over medium-high heat. (If you don't have a double boiler, set one saucepan into a slightly larger one that you've filled with ½ inch water.)
3. While the chocolate is melting, put the butter and cream cheese into a large mixing bowl. Add the powdered sugar and *cream* this mixture, using an electric mixer set on medium speed.
4. Add the melted chocolate and the milk to the creamed mixture and *beat* on medium speed until the chocolate is blended and the mixture is of spreading consistency. (If the frosting is too thick, add more milk, a few drops at a time, beating with the electric mixer until the frosting is the right consistency. If the frosting is too thin, add more powdered sugar to thicken.)

ASSEMBLING THE TORTE

1 pound cake (about 10¾ ounces), *frozen* (do not defrost!)
1 recipe (above) Chocolate Cream Cheese Frosting
½ cup apricot jam or preserves

1. With the frozen cake on its side on a cutting board, use a long-bladed knife to *cut* the cake into five even layers (see picture).

Slicing the frozen pound cake into layers.

2. Set the bottom layer of the cake on an oblong platter. Spread with ¼ cup chocolate frosting. Top with a second cake layer.
3. Spread the top of the second layer with ¼ cup apricot jam. Top with a third cake layer.
4. Spread the top of the third layer with ¼ cup chocolate frosting. Top with a fourth cake layer.
5. Spread the fourth layer with the remaining ¼ cup apricot jam. Cover with the final layer of cake, smooth side up. Brush off any crumbs from the top and sides of the cake. Frost the top and sides with the remaining chocolate frosting.
6. Refrigerate the torte until serving time.
7. At dessert time, set the torte on the dining table. Cut the torte *crosswise* into thin slices. Serve on individual dessert plates.

"LET'S TALK TURKEY" DINNER

Begin preparations about 1 hour and 5 minutes before dinnertime.

Phase	Cold Turkey Salad	Dilly Tomatoes	Chocolate Cream Cheese Frosting	Assembling the Torte
I			Step 1	
II	Steps 1–8			
III			Steps 2–4	
IV				Steps 1–6
V		Steps 1–4		
VI	Step 9			
VII				At dessert time, Step 7

"It's Greek to Me" Dinner

Serves 6

Greece! Homer, Sophocles, Euripides, Hippocrates, Athens and Sparta, the Acropolis, the Parthenon. . . .

We owe a lot to the ancient Greeks: the concept of the city-state, the beginnings of democracy, and the origins of modern medicine are just a few of the many influences that Greece has had on American government and science.

Greece has also contributed ample recipes from her unique cuisine. Because most of Greece is made up of lakes and mountains, only about one-quarter of the country can be used for orchards and fields. This terrain is better suited for raising sheep and goats than for raising cattle. That's why Nico's Lamb Kabobs are so characteristically Greek, especially when topped with the lemon-and-garlic-flavored yogurt sauce. This meal is anything but Spartan when you add the *spanakopita,* or Spinach-Cheese Pie, and the Atheneum Tomato Rice. Then, in true Middle Eastern tradition, bring out Fruits of the Acropolis Melon-Grape Tray for a light, refreshing dessert.

Dinner will take about one and a half hours from start to finish, but you'll have a fifteen-minute breaktime. So—call your family and friends to the table, and partake in this Olympian feast!

Nico's Lamb Kabobs with Greek Yogurt Sauce
Spinach-Cheese Pie   Atheneum Tomato Rice
Fruits of the Acropolis Melon-Grape Tray

Nico's Lamb Kabobs with Greek Yogurt Sauce

If possible, accompany the kabobs with pieces of the round, flat pita bread to soak up any leftover sauce.

GREEK YOGURT SAUCE

     1 container (8 ounces) plain yogurt
¼ to ½ teaspoon garlic salt
     1 lemon wedge (¼ lemon)

NICO'S LAMB KABOBS

    2 pounds ground lamb (or 1 pound ground lamb and 1 pound ground beef)
1¼ teaspoons salt
 ¼ teaspoon pepper
  1 medium or large egg (or 2 small eggs)
  1 medium onion

1. Preheat the oven to 350°F.
2. Empty the yogurt into a small serving bowl and sprinkle the garlic salt over it.
3. Remove any seeds from the lemon wedge with the tip of a small, sharp knife. Using your fingers, press the lemon wedge to squeeze out as much juice as possible over the yogurt. *Stir* the yogurt mixture with a spoon to combine ingredients.
4. Cover the yogurt sauce with plastic wrap and refrigerate until serving time.
5. Place the lamb (or combination of lamb and beef), salt, and pepper in a large mixing bowl. Break the egg into the bowl over the meat and seasonings.

6. On a cutting board, use a sharp knife to *cut* off the ends of the onion. *Peel* off the dry outer skin. Discard the skin and ends of the onion. Use the sharp knife to *mince* the onion. Add the minced onion to the bowl with the meat. Stir with a large spoon to thoroughly combine ingredients.
7. Shape the lamb mixture into balls about the size of Ping-Pong balls. Thread the balls onto several skewers. Set the skewers on a rack over a broiling pan or shallow baking pan.
8. Place the kabobs in the oven and *bake* for about 35 minutes.
9. Using potholders, carefully remove the pan of kabobs from the oven. (Be sure to hold the pan under the kabobs securely, because it will contain hot fat drippings from the meat, and a spill could cause a severe burn.) Then hold the gripper end of each skewer with a potholder. With a fork in your other hand, carefully slide off the lamb kabobs onto individual dinner plates. Set on the dining table.
10. Take the yogurt sauce from the refrigerator and discard the plastic wrap. Spoon yogurt sauce generously over the lamb kabobs.

Spinach-Cheese Pie

In Greece, this pie is made using paper-thin layers of dough called *phyllo*. Phyllo pastry can often be found in the frozen foods section of large supermarkets and in specialty food shops in the United States, but the Greeks make their own phyllo. For convenience, our recipe does not call for phyllo pastry, but the results are equally delicious.

 2 teaspoons butter or margarine
 1 package (10 ounces) frozen chopped spinach
 8 ounces feta (Greek) cheese (or substitute 8 ounces Cheddar cheese)
 1 pint (2 cups) small-curd cottage cheese
   several sprigs fresh parsley
 4 medium or large eggs (or 6 small eggs)
 1/3 cup flour
 1/2 teaspoon salt
 1/2 teaspoon pepper

1. Preheat the oven to 350°F.

2. *Grease* a 9-inch-square pan with the 2 teaspoons butter or margarine. Set aside.
3. Prepare the spinach according to package directions, using a medium saucepan with a lid.
4. While the spinach is cooking, *crumble* the feta cheese into a large bowl. (If you are using Cheddar cheese, *grate* the Cheddar cheese into the large bowl.)
5. When the spinach is cooked, *drain* it in a colander or strainer. Use a large spoon to press out any excess liquid. Place the well-drained spinach in the bowl with the feta (or Cheddar) cheese.
6. Add the cottage cheese to the bowl with the spinach and feta cheese.
7. On a cutting board, use a paring knife or kitchen scissors to *mince* enough parsley leaves to yield 2 tablespoons. Add the minced parsley to the spinach and cheeses.
8. Break the eggs into a medium bowl. Add the flour, salt, and pepper to the eggs. Use a wire whisk (or an eggbeater) to *beat* the ingredients until smooth and well blended. Add this egg mixture to the bowl with the spinach-cheese mixture. Use a large spoon to combine ingredients.
9. Pour the mixture into the buttered baking pan and spread the top evenly with a rubber scraper.
10. *Bake* for 1 hour, or until a table knife inserted into the center of the pie comes out clean.
11. Using potholders, carefully remove the pie from the oven and let it cool for a few minutes to set.
12. With a knife, *cut* the pie into 9 squares (3 inches by 3 inches). Use a wide spatula to carefully lift out the spinach squares onto serving plates.

Atheneum Tomato Rice

The Greeks frequently use a tomato base when preparing rice.

   1½ cups water
       a few sprigs fresh parsley (or 1 teaspoon dried parsley)
    2 beef bouillon cubes
    1 can (8 ounces) stewed tomatoes
    1 cup converted rice

1. In a medium saucepan with a lid, bring the water to a *rapid boil* over high heat.
2. While the water is reaching a boil, on a cutting board use a paring knife or kitchen scissors to *mince* enough fresh parsley to yield 2 tablespoons. Set aside.
3. When the water has reached a boil, add the bouillon cubes to the water. Continue boiling until the cubes *dissolve*. (You can speed this up by breaking up the bouillon cubes with a fork while they are in the boiling water.)
4. Add the stewed tomatoes (undrained), the 2 tablespoons of fresh parsley (or the 1 teaspoon of dried parsley), and the rice to the water. *Stir* the ingredients a couple of times. Then cover the saucepan with the lid and reduce the heat just low enough to maintain a *simmer*.
5. Simmer, covered, for 25 minutes, or until the liquid is absorbed by the rice.
6. Fluff the rice with a fork and transfer it to a serving bowl.

Fruits of the Acropolis Melon-Grape Tray

A delicious and light way to end a hearty meal, and very much in the Greek tradition.

1 honeydew melon, chilled
1 pound grapes (green or purple, or a combination of the two)
1 lemon

1. On a cutting board, use a large, sharp knife to carefully *cut* the melon in half *lengthwise*. Use a spoon to remove the seeds from each melon half.
2. Use the sharp knife to cut each melon half lengthwise into 3 equal wedges. You should now have 6 wedges of melon.
3. Find an attractive, medium-size tray or large platter of any shape. Arrange the melon wedges on the tray in an attractive pattern (see picture).
4. Rinse the grapes with cold water. Carefully pat dry with paper towels. Using a small knife, or a grapes scissors (yes, there are such things!), or a kitchen scissors, cut the grape stems into

Fruits of the Acropolis arranged attractively on serving tray.

several small clusters of grapes. Arrange the grape clusters among the melon wedges.

5. On the cutting board, use the knife to cut the lemon in half lengthwise. Then cut each lemon half into 3 lengthwise slices, yielding 6 wedges in all. Arrange the lemon wedges on the melon-grape tray. Cover with plastic wrap and refrigerate until serving time.

6. At dessert time, remove the fruit tray from the refrigerator and place on the dining table, along with 6 individual small dessert plates. Each person should help himself or herself to a wedge of melon, some grapes, and a lemon wedge. We suggest squeezing lemon juice over the melon for a delightfully tart taste that is typically Greek.

"IT'S GREEK TO ME" DINNER

Begin preparations about 1½ hours before dinnertime.

Phase	Nico's Lamb Kabobs With Greek Yogurt Sauce	Spinach-Cheese Pie	Atheneum Tomato Rice	Fruits of the Acropolis Melon-Grape Tray
I		Steps 1–10		
II	Steps 2–8			
III			Steps 1–5	
IV				Steps 1–5

15-MINUTE BREAKTIME

Phase	Nico's Lamb Kabobs With Greek Yogurt Sauce	Spinach-Cheese Pie	Atheneum Tomato Rice	Fruits of the Acropolis Melon-Grape Tray
V		Step 11		
VI	Steps 9–10	Step 12	Step 6	
VII				At dessert time, Step 6

"Hard Day's Night" Dinner

Serves 6

From time to time, everyone has a hard day. A frozen TV dinner won't be satisfying—you feel you deserve something better, something homemade and tasty. But who wants to spend a lot of time in the kitchen?

We have put together a menu for just such a hard day's night. You will have to begin preparations about two and a half hours before dinner, but you do get three long breaktimes. Consider meditating in your easy chair, soaking in the bathtub.

The Jiffy Ham and Cheese Bake is rich, soufflélike sandwiches. We complement them with Instant Polka-dotted Asparagus and a salad medley of Berry Easy Fruit Cups. For dessert, enjoy Simple as Pie Brownies with your evening beverage. Troubles will melt away with every bite, and you're bound to forget that this has been a hard day's night.

Jiffy Ham and Cheese Bake
Instant Polka-dotted Asparagus   Berry Easy Fruit Cups
Simple as Pie Brownies

Jiffy Ham and Cheese Bake

This recipe is ideal for the person who is on the go. If you prefer, prepare Steps 1–6 the night before or the morning of your hard day. With these steps done, you'll need only 1½ hours later on to assemble the rest of the dinner, and most of that time will be for breaktimes. Just proceed with Phase II on the chart.

> 12 slices white bread
> 2 tablespoons butter, softened
> 6 slices American cheese
> 6 thin slices ham
>   mustard, to taste
> 4 medium or large eggs
> 3 cups milk
> ½ teaspoon garlic powder

1. On a cutting board, using a sharp knife, remove the crusts from all 12 slices of bread. (You might *grate* the crusts in your blender and store the crumbs in the freezer for recipes using bread crumbs. Or toss the crusts out as a treat for the birds.)
2. Butter 6 slices of bread, and place them butter side down in a 13-by-9-inch baking dish.
3. Place 1 slice of cheese on each slice of bread in the baking dish. Then cover each cheese slice with a ham slice.
4. Spread the remaining 6 slices of bread with mustard and place the bread, mustard side down, on the ham slices to form sandwiches.
5. Break the eggs into a large mixing bowl. Add the milk and the garlic powder and *beat* well with a fork or wire whisk.
6. Pour the egg-milk mixture over the sandwiches. Cover the pan with plastic wrap and refrigerate for at least 1 hour.
7. Preheat the oven to 325°F.
8. Remove the dish of sandwiches from the refrigerator and discard the plastic wrap. *Bake* the sandwiches in the oven for 1¼ hours.
9. Using potholders, carefully remove the pan from the oven and set on a warming pad. To serve, use a wide spatula to lift out the sandwiches onto the dinner plates.

Instant Polka-dotted Asparagus

Flecks of pimiento make these asparagus spears extra special.

  1 chicken bouillon cube
  1 package (10 ounces) frozen asparagus spears
  1 tablespoon chopped pimiento (or half of a 2-ounce jar,
     drained; or buy a 2-ounce jar of large pimiento pieces and
     dice)
  1 tablespoon butter or margarine

1. In a large skillet that has a tight-fitting lid, bring one cup of water to a *boil* over high heat.
2. Add the bouillon cube and *stir* with a fork until the cube *dissolves.*
3. Carefully add the asparagus spears to the boiling water.
4. When the water returns to a boil, reduce the heat to medium-low. Cover the skillet and *simmer* for about 8 minutes, or until the spears are *fork-tender.* (After a few minutes of cooking, it is a good idea to remove the lid and separate with a fork any spears that are still frozen together.)
5. Use a fork or slotted spoon to carefully lift the asparagus spears from the skillet to a serving dish.
6. *Drain* enough chopped pimiento from the jar to measure out 1 tablespoon. Sprinkle the pimiento pieces over the asparagus.
7. *Dot* the asparagus spears with the butter.

Berry Easy Fruit Cups

Try any combination of fruits, taking advantage of fruits in season. Consider grapes, peaches, pears, pineapple, blueberries.

  1 package (10 ounces) frozen strawberry slices, thawed
  1 medium or large apple
  1 medium or large orange (we suggest a navel orange, because
     it is seedless and easy to peel)
  1 banana, any size

1. Empty the carton of strawberries with their syrup into a medium-size bowl.

2. Wash the apple under cold water. On a cutting board, use a paring knife to quarter the apple. Remove the seeds and core parts and *cut* each apple quarter into about 6 pieces. Add the apple pieces to the bowl with the berries.
3. *Peel* the orange and separate it into sections. Cut each orange section in half and add to the bowl with the berries and apple pieces.
4. Remove the peel from the banana. *Slice* the banana and add to the fruit bowl.
5. Gently combine the fruits with a large spoon. Cover the fruit bowl with plastic wrap to retain the vitamins, and refrigerate.
6. At serving time, divide the fruit among 6 small fruit cups and serve as a salad.

Simple as Pie Brownies

A brownie pie that really is simple as pie.

    1 tablespoon butter or margarine
    2 packets (1 ounce each) liquid chocolate, unsweetened*
  ½ cup butter or margarine, softened
    1 cup sugar
    1 teaspoon vanilla
    2 medium or large eggs
  ½ cup regular enriched white flour
  ½ cup chopped walnuts, pecans, or other nuts (optional)
     powdered sugar

1. Preheat the oven to 325°F.
2. *Grease* a 9-inch pie plate (or an 8-inch-square pan) with the 1 tablespoon butter.
3. Put the unopened chocolate packets in a bowl of warm water to soften the chocolate. Set aside.
4. With an electric mixer, *cream* the ½ cup butter, the sugar, and the vanilla in a large mixing bowl.

---

* If liquid chocolate is not available, add 2 additional tablespoons of softened butter to the ½ cup butter in Step 4, and substitute 6 tablespoons unsweetened cocoa for the chocolate in Step 6.

Rubber Scraper

5. Add the eggs to the creamed mixture. *Beat* with the electric mixer on medium-to-high speed for 3 minutes.
6. Remove the chocolate packets from the water. Cut open the packets and squeeze the chocolate directly into the bowl with the batter. Beat with the electric mixer on medium speed to *blend* in the chocolate.
7. Using a rubber scraper, scrape the bowl and beaters.
8. Use a wooden spoon to *stir* in the flour and nuts. Continue to stir until all the ingredients are well blended.
9. Pour the batter into the prepared pan. *Bake* for 30 to 35 minutes. (Undercook slightly if you like chewy brownies.)
10. Using potholders, remove the pan from the oven and set on a wire rack to cool.
11. Sprinkle the brownies with powdered sugar and *cut* into wedges. (Cut into bars, if using a square pan.) Serve warm or cooled.

"HARD DAY'S NIGHT" DINNER

Start Phase I about 2½ hours before dinnertime.

Phase	Jiffy Ham and Cheese Bake	Instant Polka-dotted Asparagus	Berry Easy Fruit Cups	Simple as Pie Brownies
I	Steps 1–6			
40-MINUTE BREAKTIME				
II				Steps 1–9
III	Steps 7–8			
30-MINUTE BREAKTIME				
IV				Step 10
V			Steps 1–5	
20-MINUTE BREAKTIME				
VI		Steps 1–7		
VII	Step 9		Step 6	
VIII				At dessert time, Step 11

"Surprise" Dinner

Serves 6

This menu deserves its title because every recipe contains a surprise. Hidden in the meat loaf are hard-boiled eggs. This surprise adds color, taste, interest, and important protein to an otherwise ordinary dish. The surprise in the foil packages is baked potatoes, so delicious that it's hard to believe how surprisingly easy they are to prepare. Water chestnuts are the surprise element in the peas—a "sure-prize" recipe for the vegetable category. Finally, a homemade caramel sauce transforms plain ice cream into a "surpr-ice-cream" dessert special.

Plan to start preparations about one hour and forty-five minutes before dinnertime. You will be in the kitchen during most of the first hour, but then you will have a forty-five-minute breaktime. Use this time to call a friend, write a letter, or do your yoga exercises. Then return to the kitchen to prepare the peas. If you follow our chart carefully, the peas will be done just when you take the meat loaf and potatoes from the oven.

You'll be surprised at how often you will want to make this simple and delicious all-American dinner for your family and friends.

Surprise Meat Loaf
Surprisingly Easy Baked Potatoes   *Sure-Prize Peas*
Caramel Surpr-Ice-Cream

Surprise Meat Loaf

If you don't already have hard-boiled eggs in the refrigerator, cook 2 or 3 while you're eating breakfast that morning.

        10 pimiento-stuffed green olives (optional)
         2 pounds lean ground beef (Since lean ground beef has
            less fat content than regular ground beef, there is less
            shrinkage during cooking. So although lean ground beef
            is more expensive, it is a better value.)
         2 eggs, any size
        ¾ cup ketchup
      1½ cups bread crumbs, soft or dry
        ½ cup warm water or evaporated milk
         1 envelope (from a 2¾-ounce box of 2 envelopes) dried
            onion soup mix
   2 to 3 hard-boiled eggs
         2 strips bacon
         1 can (8 ounces) tomato sauce

1. Preheat the oven to 350°F.
2. On a cutting board, using a paring knife, quarter the olives. Then place the olive quarters in a large bowl. Add the meat, uncooked eggs, ketchup, bread crumbs, water or evaporated milk, and onion soup mix.
3. Using a wooden spoon, combine the ingredients until well blended.
4. Put about half the meat mixture into a loaf pan (about 9 inches by 5 inches by 3 inches). Make a hollow nest for each hard-boiled egg.
5. Remove and discard the shells from the hard-boiled eggs. Place an egg in each nest. (See picture.)
6. Cover the eggs with the remaining meat mixture. Pat down.
7. Place the strips of bacon *lengthwise* on top of the meat loaf. Then pour over the tomato sauce.
8. *Bake* for 1½ hours.
9. Using potholders, remove the meat loaf from the oven. *Cut* the meat loaf *crosswise* into thick slices. Using a wide spatula, carefully lift the slices from the loaf pan and arrange them on a serving platter.

Placing the hard-boiled eggs in their "nests" for Surprise Meat Loaf.

Surprisingly Easy Baked Potatoes

Did you know that potatoes are called "apples of the earth"?

6 medium baking potatoes
1 tablespoon butter or margarine
    extra butter or margarine
    salt and pepper

1. Preheat the oven to 350°F.
2. Under cold running water, scrub the potatoes with a vegetable brush to remove dirt.
3. Using a paring knife with a sharp tip, remove any eyes from the potatoes. (Do this by making a small circular cut around the eye.)
4. Rub the potatoes with the 1 tablespoon butter or margarine.
5. *Cut* off 6 pieces of aluminum foil large enough to enclose a potato. Wrap each potato snugly in a piece of foil.
6. Using a fork, prick each potato through the foil in several places. (This will allow steam to escape, and prevent any potato explosions.)
7. *Bake* for about 1¼ hours, or until *fork-tender.*
8. Using potholders, remove the potatoes from the oven. Place a foil-wrapped baked potato on each dinner plate. Pass the butter, salt, and pepper.

Sure-Prize Peas

The water chestnuts add a pleasant crunch.

>   1 can water chestnuts (Water chestnuts come in several
>   different can sizes, but the 8-ounce size seems to be the
>   most common. Buy the smallest can size that your store
>   stocks.)
>   2 packages (10 ounces each, or 1 20-ounce bag) frozen
>   peas
> 2 to 3 tablespoons butter or margarine
>   salt and pepper

1. *Drain* the water chestnuts. *Slice* enough water chestnuts to fill
   ½ cup. (Save the remainder in a covered container in the
   refrigerator for your next salad or casserole.)
2. In a medium saucepan with a lid, prepare the peas in salted
   water according to package directions.
3. Drain the peas in a colander or strainer.
4. Return the peas to the saucepan. Add the butter, water chestnuts, and salt and pepper to taste. Toss gently to combine
   ingredients.
5. Keep warm over low heat. When ready to serve, transfer the
   peas and water chestnuts to a serving dish.

Caramel Surpr-Ice-Cream

If you have a sweet tooth, you'll love this dessert!

>   2 tablespoons butter (do not substitute margarine)
>   ½ cup brown sugar, *firmly packed*
>   ¼ cup light cream (or half-and-half)
>   ½ teaspoon vanilla
>   1 quart vanilla or butter pecan ice cream

1. *Melt* the butter in a small saucepan over medium-low heat.
2. *Stir* in the brown sugar. Then remove the saucepan from the
   heat.

3. Gradually add the light cream, stirring until the mixture is well blended.
4. Return the saucepan to the heat for one minute, stirring constantly.
5. Remove the saucepan from the heat and add the vanilla. Set aside.
6. About five minutes before serving dessert, warm the sauce over medium-low heat, stirring frequently (don't let the sauce *scorch*).
7. Put a generous scoop of ice cream in each of 6 dessert bowls. Spoon the warm caramel sauce over the ice cream and serve at once.

"SURPRISE" DINNER

Begin Phase I about 1 hour and 45 minutes before dinnertime.

Phase	Surprise Meat Loaf	Surprisingly Easy Baked Potatoes	Sure-Prize Peas	Caramel Surpr-Ice-Cream
I	Steps 1–8			
II		Steps 2–7		
III				Steps 1–5

45-MINUTE BREAKTIME

Phase	Surprise Meat Loaf	Surprisingly Easy Baked Potatoes	Sure-Prize Peas	Caramel Surpr-Ice-Cream
IV			Steps 1–5	
V	Step 9	Step 8		
VI				At dessert time, Steps 6–7

"Sorry, Charlie!" Dinner

Serves 6

No need to apologize to Charlie, or to anyone else, for this dinner. Tonight's menu features Star-Kissed Tuna Casserole, the creamiest, crunchiest, and most delicious tuna dish we've ever eaten. While it bakes in the same oven with Charlie's Carrot Stix, you can prepare the Tomato-Cucumber-Onion Wheel and the pretty Pineapple-Cherry Kabob dessert.

Begin preparations about one hour and fifteen minutes before you plan to eat. Don't count on a breaktime, though, unless you're a superfast worker.

Show your good taste and serve Sorry, Charlie! Dinner to your family and friends often. This meal is simple to prepare, tasty, nutritious, and easy on the budget. And it's not only in good taste, but—really, Charlie—it tastes good too!

Star-Kissed Tuna Casserole
Charlie's Carrot Stix   *Tomato-Cucumber-Onion Wheel*
Pineapple-Cherry Kabobs

Star-Kissed Tuna Casserole

Delicious! Not your typical ho-hum tuna dish.

3 quarts water
1 tablespoon salt
1 tablespoon oil
1 teaspoon butter or margarine
8 ounces flat, wide noodles
1 cup (½ pint) dairy sour cream
1 can (10½ ounces) cream of mushroom soup
1 can (8 ounces) water chestnuts
2 cans (about 7 ounces each) tuna fish
2 cans (3 ounces each) French-fried onions
  parsley sprigs for garnish (optional)

1. Preheat the oven to 350°F.
2. In a large pot, bring the water, salt, and oil to a *rapid boil* over high heat.
3. Meanwhile, *grease* a 2- to 2½-quart casserole with the 1 teaspoon butter. (Choose a casserole that has a lid, or use aluminum foil secured over the top of the casserole.)
4. Carefully add the noodles to the rapidly boiling water. (If the water begins to boil over, reduce the heat, but always maintain a boil.)
5. *Stir* the noodles frequently with a long-handled spoon to prevent sticking. Boil just until the noodles are *al dente*, approximately 7 to 8 minutes.
6. While the noodles are cooking, combine the sour cream and soup in a large bowl.
7. *Drain* the water chestnuts. On a cutting board, use a sharp knife to carefully *slice* the water chestnuts. Add to the sour cream–soup mixture.
8. Drain the two cans of tuna of any excess oil or water. Add the tuna to the sour cream–soup mixture.
9. Drain the noodles in a colander. Add the drained noodles to the mixture in the bowl.
10. Add one of the cans of French-fried onions to the mixture in the bowl. Gently *fold* with a wooden spoon to combine ingredients.

11. Transfer the entire mixture into the buttered casserole. Place the French-fried onions from the remaining can on top of the mixture.
12. Cover the casserole with the lid or a piece of heavy-duty aluminum foil. *Bake* for 25 minutes.
13. Remove the lid or foil cover. Continue to bake, uncovered, for 5 more minutes.
14. Using potholders, remove the casserole from the oven. *Garnish* the top of the casserole with parsley sprigs, if desired. Place the casserole on a trivet or hot pad.

Charlie's Carrot Stix

These baked carrots should be crisp, so be careful not to over-cook.

    12 medium-size, fresh carrots
     1 cup water
     1 teaspoon salt
     4 tablespoons (½ stick) butter or margarine

1. Preheat the oven to 350° F.
2. *Peel* the carrots with a vegetable peeler.
3. On a cutting board, *cut* off and discard the carrot ends with a paring knife. Then cut each carrot in half *crosswise*. Next, cut each carrot half *lengthwise* into strips.
4. Arrange the carrot "stix" in a shallow casserole that has a lid. Pour the water over the carrots. Sprinkle with the salt and *dot* with the butter.
5. Cover the casserole with the lid and *bake* for 1 hour.
6. Using potholders, remove the casserole from the oven and place on a hot pad or trivet.

Tomato-Cucumber-Onion Wheel

A tasty and colorful salad medley that is low in calories.

    2 to 3 medium-size, ripe tomatoes
         1 large, fresh cucumber

2 large slices from a medium-large Bermuda or sweet onion
oil and vinegar or Italian salad dressing (your own or
store-bought), optional

1. Rinse the tomatoes and cucumber under cold water. Gently
   pat dry with paper towels.
2. On a cutting board, using a sharp knife, *cut* each tomato *cross-wise* into several slices. Cut out and discard the core section.
3. Do not *pare* the cucumber. (Did you know that the green
   cucumber skin contains a large amount of vitamins?) Use the
   sharp knife or a paring knife to cut the cucumber crosswise
   into fairly thin slices. Discard the end pieces.
4. Cut two center slices crosswise from the onion. Discard the
   dry outer skin from the slices. Separate each onion slice into
   rings. (See picture, page 47.) (Wrap the remaining onion in
   plastic wrap, refrigerate, and save for another use.)
5. On a round dinner plate, arrange overlapping slices of tomato,
   cucumber, and onion. Cover with plastic wrap and store in the
   refrigerator until serving time.
6. Take the vegetable wheel from the refrigerator and remove
   the plastic wrap. Serve with dressing, if desired.

Pineapple-Cherry Kabobs

Light, refreshing, and festive enough to serve at parties. If you
prefer fresh fruit to the maraschino cherries, try substituting
strawberries or green or purple grapes.

1 fresh pineapple
1 small jar maraschino cherries
round toothpicks

1. Place the pineapple on its side on a cutting board. Very carefully, use a large, sharp knife to halve the pineapple, starting
   at the stem end of the fruit and cutting right through the
   leaves. (See diagram A.)
2. Place a pineapple half, fruit side up, on a cutting board. Use
   the sharp knife to *cut* it in half *lengthwise*, again going
   through the fruit and the leaves. Repeat with the other pine-

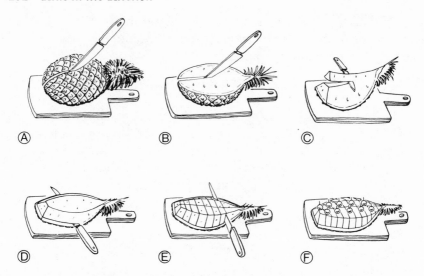

Ⓐ   Ⓑ   Ⓒ

Ⓓ   Ⓔ   Ⓕ

Steps in preparing the pineapple for Pineapple-Cherry Kabobs.

apple half. You should now have 4 pineapple quarters. (See diagram B.)

3. Use a smaller knife (or a paring knife) to remove the tough core from each pineapple quarter. (See diagram C.)

4. With a grapefruit knife, or a narrow, long-bladed kitchen knife, carefully separate the fruit from the rind, but do not remove it from the rind. (See diagram D.)

5. *Slice* each quarter in half lengthwise down to the rind, and then slice each quarter *crosswise* into sections approximately ½-inch wide. (See diagram E.)

6. *Skewer* every other pineapple section with a toothpick, placing a cherry on top as you go. (See diagram F.)

7. Arrange the 4 pineapple quarters on a large serving plate. Refrigerate until serving time.

8. Remove the kabob platter from the refrigerator and serve with small dessert plates.

"SORRY, CHARLIE!" DINNER

Start preparations about 1 hour and 15 minutes before dinnertime.

Phase	Star-Kissed Tuna Casserole	Charlie's Carrot Stix	Tomato-Cucumber-Onion Wheel	Pineapple-Cherry Kabobs
I		Steps 1–5		
II	Steps 2–12			
III			Steps 1–5	
IV				Steps 1–7
V	Step 13			
VI	Step 14	Step 6	Step 6	
VII				At dessert time, Step 8

"Mexicali" Dinner

Serves 6

This is a fun meal with a Mexican flair. Preparation is easy and should take only forty to forty-five minutes from start to finish. While Roberto's Meat Sauce and the Just Plain Rice are cooking, you can set the table and prepare all the condiments (Los Condimentos). Add a cold beverage and bread (corn bread is a delicious choice) and cap the meal with a light dessert, such as our refreshing Lemon-Mint Olé.

Mexicali Dinner can easily be adapted for large groups or parties; simply double or triple each recipe to accommodate the number of guests. Roberto's Meat Sauce can be prepared a day ahead, stored in the refrigerator, and reheated in a large pot or Crock-Pot before serving. Just Plain Rice, too, can be made in advance, refrigerated, and reheated, covered, in a warm oven. All the Condimentos, except for the Tortilla Chips, can be prepared earlier and stored inside airtight containers in the refrigerator. Keep the crushed Tortilla Chips in a plastic bag at room temperature. Your party will be a huge success, and we're sure that all your guests will exclaim, *"¡Maravilloso!"*

Mexicali Taco Bowl
Roberto's Meat Sauce   Just Plain Rice
Los Condimentos
Lemon-Mint Olé

Mexicali Taco Bowl

ROBERTO'S MEAT SAUCE

For the chili lover, add a can of drained red kidney beans after Step 4.

    1 pound ground beef
    2 cans (15¼ ounces each) Sloppy Joe
  ⅓ cup ketchup
 1½ teaspoons chili powder (or more if you like a hot sauce, but be careful not to overdo)

1. Heat a large skillet over medium-high heat, until a drop of water splashed on the skillet spatters.
2. Place the beef in the skillet and cook until brown, stirring frequently with a fork to break up the meat chunks.
3. *Drain* the fat off the meat.
4. *Stir* in the two cans of Sloppy Joe, the ketchup, and the chili powder. Add kidney beans, if desired.
5. *Simmer* uncovered over low heat for 30 minutes.
6. Keep warm over lowest heat until ready to serve.

JUST PLAIN RICE

We feel that converted rice is far superior to instant rice in texture and flavor. It is just as easy to prepare and well worth the extra minutes of cooking time.

 2½ cups water
    1 cup raw converted rice
    1 teaspoon salt
    1 tablespoon butter or margarine

1. In a medium saucepan over high heat, bring the water to a *rapid boil.*
2. *Stir* in the rice, salt, and butter or margarine.
3. Cover the saucepan with a lid. Reduce heat to low and *simmer* for 25 minutes.
4. Remove the saucepan from the heat and let stand, covered, 5

to 15 minutes, or until ready to serve (all water should be absorbed by the rice). Fluff with a fork.

LOS CONDIMENTOS

A. *Cheddar Cheese Bowl*

6 to 8 ounces cheddar cheese

1. *Grate* Cheddar cheese, using a grater or a blender. (Did you know that hard cheese can be successfully grated in the blender? First, make sure that the cheese is firm from refrigeration. Then, *cut* the cheese into small chunks and grate in the blender, a few chunks at a time. Be very careful not to overblend, or the cheese will be creamy.)
2. Transfer the grated cheese to a small serving dish.

B. *Tomato Bowl*

2 to 3 medium or large tomatoes

1. Rinse the tomatoes under cold water. With a paring knife, *cut* a circle about ¼-inch deep around the tomato stem. Remove and discard the stem piece.
2. *Chop* or *dice* the tomatoes into small pieces.
3. Transfer the chopped tomatoes to a small serving dish.

C. *Lettuce Bowl*

¼ to ⅓ head of iceberg lettuce

1. *Cut* a wedge from the head of lettuce, using a sharp knife.
2. On a cutting board, use the sharp knife to cut thin slices from the long side of the lettuce wedge, thereby *shredding* it. (See picture.)
3. Transfer the shredded lettuce to a small serving bowl.

Shredding the lettuce wedge for Mexicali Taco Bowl.

D. Tortilla Chip Bowl

1 package (5½ ounces) tortilla chips

1. While they are still in the unopened bag, gently *crush* the tortilla chips with your hands, until pieces are small enough to serve with a tablespoon.
2. Transfer the crushed chips to a small bowl.

E. Onion Bowl (*Optional*)

1 medium onion

1. On a cutting board, using a sharp knife, *cut* off both ends of the onion. Remove the dry outer skin. Discard both the ends and the skin.
2. Cut the onion in half and lay each half flat side down. *Chop* both onion halves (see picture, page 17).
3. Transfer the diced onion to a small dish.

F. Avocado Bowl (*Optional*)

1 medium avocado
½ lemon

1. On a cutting board, use a sharp knife to *cut* the avocado in half *lengthwise*. Separate into 2 sections. Remove the large pit. Use the tip of the knife to pull off the tough outer skin from the avocado sections. Place the 2 avocado sections flat side down on a cutting board. *Dice* the avocado fruit by cutting lengthwise into strips, then *crosswise* into small pieces (see picture, page 128). Add the diced avocado to the salad bowl.
2. Transfer the diced avocado to a small serving dish. Squeeze the juice from the lemon half over the avocado and toss gently with a spoon until all the pieces are well coated. (The lemon juice will prevent the avocado fruit from turning brown.)

FINAL ASSEMBLY OF TACO BOWL DINNER

1. Divide the Just Plain Rice among 6 individual plates or soup bowls.

2. Using a ladle, spoon Roberto's Meat Sauce over the Just Plain Rice.
3. Pass Los Condimentos, letting each person help himself or herself.

Lemon-Mint Olé

The tartness of lemon and freshness of mint offer a refreshing counter to the hot chili taste of Roberto's Meat Sauce.

 1 quart lemon sherbet
 crème de menthe syrup (This nonalcoholic syrup comes in an 8-ounce bottle and can usually be found in the ice cream toppings section of large supermarkets. Or use ⅓ cup green mint jelly that has been melted over low heat.)
 fresh mint leaves (optional)

1. Scoop a generous portion of lemon sherbet into each of 6 dessert bowls.
2. Top each scoop with 1 to 2 teaspoons of mint syrup.
3. *Garnish* with fresh mint leaves, if available.

"MEXICALI" DINNER

Begin Phase I about 40 to 45 minutes before dinnertime.

Phase	Roberto's Meat Sauce	Just Plain Rice	Los Condimentos	Lemon-Mint Olé
I	Steps 1–5			
II		Steps 1–3		
III			Steps A, B, C, D; E and F, optional	
IV	Step 6	Step 4		
V	FINAL ASSEMBLY			
VI				At dessert time, Steps 1–3

"Stir-fry" Dinner

Serves 6

During the last twenty years, Americans have shown a wonderful new interest in Chinese cooking. Many small towns now boast of at least one Chinese restaurant, bookstores offer a large selection of books on Chinese cooking, vocational schools list classes in the Chinese culinary arts, and most large supermarkets have a complete section just for Oriental foods.

A Chinese friend who teaches Chinese cooking to Americans once told us that it takes at least three years of apprenticeship before qualifying as a chef. She said that most of that time is devoted to learning how to cut foods properly. The correct preparation of foods is extremely important because fuel is scarce in China, and cooking time must be brief. The stir-fry method of cooking makes efficient use of fuel, which is why it is so popular in China. Meats and vegetables are cut at an angle to expose as much surface area as possible. Then they are stir-fried for a very short time over high heat until every piece of food has touched the hot *wok* or pan for just a few moments. The foods are removed from the heat when the meat is just cooked through and the vegetables are still crisp and unwilted.

Tonight's dinner provides you with the opportunity to test your own culinary abilities with Stir-fried Chicken Livers and

Vegetables and Chinese Boiled Rice. We like to add prepared frozen miniature egg rolls (or canned noodles) for extra taste and crunch, but these are optional. We do strongly recommend, however, that you accompany our unique dessert, Peking Almond Float, with crispy fortune cookies.

This meal won't take you three years to learn to do properly, but do allow an hour and forty-five minutes, because the dessert must have time to set. You will have two breaktimes though, to browse through some history books and read up on the ancient Chinese dynasties. Be sure to return to the kitchen in time for the final assembly of ingredients.

We feel that Stir-fry Dinner is special enough to serve to company. You might even want to try your luck using chopsticks. But whether you use chopsticks or a fork, we know that this authentic menu will cause a big stir in your house whenever you make it for family or friends.

Stir-fried Chicken Livers and Vegetables
Chinese Boiled Rice
Peking Almond Float

Stir-fried Chicken Livers and Vegetables

If you don't care for chicken livers, you can substitute chicken. Discard the skin and bones from 3 whole chicken breasts, uncooked. Then *cut* the chicken into thin strips.

   1 package (6 ounces) frozen pea pods
   1 can (8 ounces) water chestnuts
   2 green onions (scallions)
   ½ pound fresh mushrooms
   1½ pounds chicken livers
   4 tablespoons oil
   2 tablespoons soy sauce
   2 teaspoons corn starch
   2 teaspoons sugar
   ½ teaspoon ginger
   ½ teaspoon salt
   ½ cup (about 2½ ounces) almonds or cashews (optional)

1. Remove the frozen pea pods from their package and place them in a large bowl.
2. *Drain* off the liquid from the can of water chestnuts. On a cutting board, use a paring knife to *cut* the water chestnuts into thirds. Place the sliced water chestnuts in the bowl with the pea pods.
3. Rinse the green onions with cold water. Pat dry with paper towels. Use the paring knife to cut off the root ends of the onions. Remove and discard any bruised or dried outer skin. Thinly *slice* the onions, including both the white and green parts. Add the onion slices to the bowl containing the pea pods and water chestnuts.
4. Put the mushrooms in a colander and wash each mushroom thoroughly with cold water. Then shake the colander to remove any excess water. Pat the mushrooms dry with paper towels.
5. On the cutting board, use the paring knife to cut off the tough ends (about ¼ inch) from the mushroom stems. Then slice the mushrooms into thirds *lengthwise,* cutting through both the cap and the stem. Add the sliced mushrooms to the bowl with the other vegetables. Set aside until Step 10.
6. Place the chicken livers in the colander and rinse under cold water. Shake the colander to remove any excess moisture. Pat the livers dry with paper towels. Place the livers on the cutting board and cut each liver in half with the paring knife. Remove any of the white membrane from the livers at this time. Then place the halved chicken livers in a medium bowl and set aside.
7. Place 2 tablespoons of the oil in a large skillet or wok (or electric fry pan or electric wok) over high heat (use a high

Electric Wok

setting if using an electric fry pan or electric wok). The oil is hot enough if it sizzles when a drop of water is splashed on it.

8. While the oil is heating, combine the soy sauce, corn starch, sugar, ginger, and salt in a small dish. Set aside until Step 11.
9. Carefully add the chicken livers to the skillet or wok. (You may have to lower the heat temporarily if the oil is spattering when the livers are first put in the pan.) Use a long-handled spoon or fork to gently *stir* the chicken livers as they fry. When all sides of the chicken livers are browned, cut into some of them with a fork to make sure that the insides are cooked and pink. If the insides are still red, cook for a couple minutes longer. When the livers are done, carefully transfer them to a bowl and set aside until Step 11.
10. Return the skillet to the stove and add the remaining 2 tablespoons of oil. (You may have to lower the heat again temporarily if the oil is spattering.) When the oil is hot, add the bowl of vegetables and the nuts, if desired. *Stir-fry* the vegetables and nuts for 3 or 4 minutes.
11. Add the stir-fried chicken livers and the soy sauce mixture to the vegetables in the skillet. Stir-fry all the ingredients for another 3 to 5 minutes, or until the food is well heated throughout.
12. Use a large serving spoon to carefully transfer the livers and vegetables to a serving dish. Serve over Chinese Boiled Rice.

Chinese Boiled Rice

This rice, known in China as *pai-fan,* is different from our other rice recipes. We think you'll like it, especially when served with stir-fried meats and vegetables.

> 2 cups long-grained enriched (not converted or instant) white rice
> 3½ cups cold water

1. Place the rice in a large 3- to 4-quart saucepan that has a tight-fitting lid. Add enough cold water from the tap to completely cover the rice. *Stir* thoroughly with a wooden spoon.

2. *Drain* the rice in a sieve or strainer. Return the drained rice to the saucepan.
3. Now add the 3½ cups fresh, cold water to the rice. Bring the rice and water to a *rapid boil* over high heat. Boil, uncovered, for 3 minutes.
4. Cover the saucepan tightly with the lid. Reduce the heat to medium-low and *simmer* 15 to 20 minutes.
5. After the rice has simmered for about 20 minutes, turn off the heat but do not uncover the saucepan. Let the rice stand untouched for 10 to 20 minutes.
6. Remove the lid from the saucepan. Use a fork to gently fluff the rice.
7. Transfer the rice to a large serving bowl and serve with Stir-fried Chicken Livers and Vegetables.

Peking Almond Float

Light, and so different. Wonderful with fortune cookies!

    2 envelopes (2 tablespoons) plain gelatin
    1 cup cold water
    2 cups whole milk
  ⅔ cup sugar
     dash of salt
    1 tablespoon almond extract
    1 can (16 ounces) mandarin oranges

1. Combine the gelatin and the cold water in a medium bowl. *Stir* with a wooden spoon until the gelatin particles are *dissolved*. Set aside.
2. Empty the milk into a medium saucepan. Bring the milk to a *boil* over medium heat, stirring constantly and watching carefully so that the milk doesn't *scorch*.
3. Pour the boiling milk into the gelatin mixture, stirring constantly.
4. Add the sugar, salt, and almond extract to the gelatin-milk mixture. Stir to *dissolve* the sugar and to combine the ingredients thoroughly.

5. Pour the mixture into a 9-inch-square pan. Place in the refrigerator to set.
6. Open the can of mandarin oranges and transfer the orange sections, with about ½ cup of the syrup, to a serving bowl. Cover with plastic wrap and refrigerate until serving time.
7. At serving time, cut the gelatin into 1-inch squares (or into diamond-shaped pieces). Divide the squares evenly among 6 dessert bowls. Remove the dish with the fruit from the refrigerator and discard the plastic wrap. Pass the oranges, to be spooned over the Almond Float.

"STIR-FRY" DINNER

Begin preparations 1 hour and 45 minutes before dinnertime.

Phase	Stir-fried Chicken Livers and Vegetables	Chinese Boiled Rice	Peking Almond Float
I			Steps 1–6
15-MINUTE BREAKTIME			
II	Steps 1–6		
III		Steps 1–4	
20-MINUTE BREAKTIME			
IV		Step 5	
V	Steps 7–12		
VI		Steps 6–7	
VII			At dessert time, Step 7

"American as Apple Pie" Dinner

Serves 6

When we think about the Fourth of July, we think of Uncle Sam, fireworks displays at public parks, parades, red, white, and blue streamers, flags flying from public buildings, sparklers, and picnics.

As everyone knows, the Declaration of Independence was signed on July 4, 1776. One year later, to commemorate this event, Philadelphia held a celebration. But it was not until 1873 —nearly one hundred years later—that Pennsylvania designated the Fourth a legal holiday. Other states quickly followed suit, and now Independence Day is America's greatest patriotic event.

To celebrate this special day, we have prepared a picnic-style menu for you to serve your family. Begin preparations about one hour and fifty minutes before dinnertime, but plan on a good half-hour breaktime to get ready for the evening's fireworks. The Patriots' Hamburgers are a cinch to prepare. We're sure that Yankee Doodle Macaroni Salad and Betsy Ross's Flag Fruit Salad will become favorite take-alongs for future picnics and potlucks. Finally, to top it all off, serve Apple Pie Americana . . . for what could be as American as apple pie?

Patriots' Hamburgers
Yankee Doodle Macaroni Salad   Betsy Ross's Flag Fruit Salad
Apple Pie Americana

Patriots' Hamburgers

Serve these hamburgers with your family's favorite fixings: shredded lettuce, tomato slices, ketchup, mustard, mayonnaise, relish, sliced sweet onion, Cheddar cheese.

  2 pounds ground chuck or extra-lean ground beef
      garlic salt
  6 hamburger buns

1. Divide the meat into 6 portions, some larger, some smaller, according to the different appetites of your family members. Shape the meat portions into patties with your hands. *Season* the patties on both sides with moderate sprinklings of garlic salt.
2. Heat a large skillet over medium-high heat until a drop of water splashed on the skillet spatters.
3. Arrange the hamburger patties in the skillet in a single layer. (If there isn't enough room for all the patties in 1 skillet, use 2 skillets.) *Fry* the hamburgers until the bottom side is well-browned.
4. Using a wide spatula, carefully turn the hamburger patties so that the uncooked side is now on the bottom of the skillet. (Some fat has probably accumulated on the bottom of the pan. Be careful that it doesn't splash—grease burns are very painful.) Fry until the second side is also well browned and the insides of the patties are done the way your family likes them.
5. While the hamburgers are frying, *slice* the buns in half *crosswise* (if not already done) and open.
6. Using the spatula, remove the patties 1 at a time and place each on a hamburger bun.

Yankee Doodle Macaroni Salad

There are countless variations of macaroni salad, but we are of-fering a standard version. Dress it up according to your family's tastes. Some suggestions: peas, pimiento, cubes of Cheddar cheese, sliced sweet gherkins, or carrots, celery, and green pep-per.

    3 quarts water
    1 tablespoon salt
    1 tablespoon oil
    1 medium or large carrot
    3 cups uncooked elbow macaroni
    2 stalks celery
    ½ green pepper
    ½ teaspoon salt
    ½ cup mayonnaise

1. In a large saucepan, bring the water, salt, and oil to a *rapid boil* over high heat.
2. While the water is reaching a boil, *peel* the carrot with a vege-table peeler. Place the pared carrot on a cutting board and *cut* off both ends with a paring knife and discard. *Slice* the carrot into ¼-inch slices. Place the carrot slices in a large salad bowl.
3. When the water has reached a rapid boil, carefully add the uncooked macaroni. (If the water begins to boil over, reduce the heat, but always maintain a boil.) Boil the macaroni for about 8 minutes or until it is *al dente. Stir* occasionally with a long-handled spoon to prevent the macaroni pieces from stick-ing together.
4. While the macaroni is cooking, wash the celery and green pep-per under cold water. Pat dry with paper towels. Remove any leaves from the celery. (Place the leaves in a plastic bag in the refrigerator to add to soup or a green salad.) Place the celery stalks on the cutting board and use the paring knife to cut off both ends from the stalks. Slice the celery into ¼-inch pieces. Add the celery slices to the carrot slices in the salad bowl.

5. Remove and discard any white seeds and stem pieces from the green pepper half. Place the pepper on the cutting board and *dice* with the paring knife. Add the pepper pieces to the salad bowl.

6. When the macaroni is al dente, empty it into a colander to *drain*. Run cold water over the macaroni in the colander to stop the cooking process and to cool the macaroni. (The macaroni should be cooled before adding the mayonnaise—otherwise, the mayonnaise will turn liquid.) Shake the macaroni gently from side to side in the colander to remove as much water as possible. Then add the drained macaroni to the vegetables in the salad bowl. Sprinkle with the ½ teaspoon salt.

7. Add the mayonnaise to the macaroni and vegetables. Use a large spoon to gently combine the ingredients. Cover the bowl with plastic wrap and refrigerate until serving time.

8. At dinnertime, remove the plastic wrap from the macaroni salad and serve.

Betsy Ross's Flag Fruit Salad

Very patriotic!

  1 large section of a watermelon (about ¼ large watermelon or ½ small watermelon)
  ½ pound seedless grapes
  ½ pint fresh blueberries

1. Set the watermelon on a large dish to catch the juice as you cut into the melon. Use a melon baller (or knife) to *cut* out bite-size balls (or chunks) from the watermelon. Place the melon pieces in a serving bowl as you go along. (Try to use the parts of the watermelon that have the fewest seeds.)

Melon Baller

2. Place the grapes in a colander. Rinse the grapes with cold water and gently pat dry with paper towels. Remove all the grapes from their stems. Place the grapes in the bowl with the watermelon.
3. Now place the blueberries in the colander. Carefully rinse under cold water. Gently pat dry with paper towels. Be sure to discard any green, dried, or bruised berries. Add the blueberries to the bowl with the watermelon and grapes. Gently toss the fruit with a large spoon to distribute the fruits evenly.
4. Cover the bowl with plastic wrap and refrigerate until serving time.
5. At serving time, discard the plastic wrap and spoon the fruit salad into 6 small bowls.

Apple Pie Americana

This apple pie has an oatmeal crust which adds a delightful crunch. And a scoop of vanilla ice cream or a dollop of whipped cream on top of a slice of warm pie would be delicious.

OATMEAL PIECRUST

    ¾ cup (1½ sticks) butter
    2 cups flour
    1 cup brown sugar, *packed*
    ½ cup regular (not instant) oatmeal
    1 teaspoon salt

APPLE PIE FILLING

    4 large or 6 medium baking apples
    ¾ cup sugar
    ¾ cup water
    1 tablespoon cornstarch
    ¼ teaspoon salt
    ½ teaspoon vanilla

1. Preheat the oven to 375°F.
2. In a small saucepan, *melt* the butter over low heat, being careful that the butter doesn't brown.
3. While the butter is melting, place the flour, brown sugar, oatmeal, and salt into a medium-size bowl.
4. Add the melted butter to the dry ingredients in the bowl and *stir* to combine thoroughly.
5. Remove 1 cup of the mixture and set aside until Step 9. Pat the remainder of the mixture over the bottom and up the sides of a 9-inch pie plate to form a crust. Set aside.
6. *Core* and *pare* the apples. On a cutting board, use a sharp knife to *slice* the apples into ¼-inch wedges. Arrange the apple wedges on the oatmeal piecrust.
7. Place the sugar, water, cornstarch, and salt in a medium saucepan. Stir to combine.
8. Bring the mixture to a *boil* over medium heat, stirring constantly. When the mixture reaches a boil, remove the saucepan from the heat. Stir in the vanilla and carefully pour the entire mixture over the apples in the pie shell. Use a rubber scraper to thoroughly remove the mixture from the sides and bottom of the saucepan. Smooth the mixture evenly over the apples.
9. With your hands, *crumble* the reserved 1 cup of crumb mixture from Step 5 evenly over the top of the pie.
10. Place the pie in the oven and *bake* for 45 minutes. (A cookie sheet placed on the oven shelf directly under the pie will catch any drippings and help keep the oven clean.)
11. Using potholders, carefully remove the pie from the oven and set on a wire rack to cool.
12. At serving time, place the pie pan on a round serving plate. *Cut* the pie into wedges and serve.

"AMERICAN AS APPLE PIE" DINNER

Begin preparations about 1 hour and 50 minutes before dinnertime.

Phase	Patriots' Hamburgers	Yankee Doodle Macaroni Salad	Betsy Ross's Flag Fruit Salad	Apple Pie Americana
I				Steps 1–10
II		Steps 1–7		
III			Steps 1–4	
IV				Step 11
30-MINUTE BREAKTIME				
V	Steps 1–5			
VI	Step 6	Step 8	Step 5	
VII				At dessert time, Step 12

"*Luau*" *Dinner*

Serves 6

HAWAIIAN ISLANDS QUIZ

1. Hawaii is the southernmost island in a chain of islands that spreads out in _____ for 1,600 miles.

   (a) the Mediterranean
   (b) the Pacific Ocean
   (c) the Indian Ocean
   (d) Lake Placid

2. About one thousand years ago, Polynesians came to Hawaii in outrigger canoes from the South Sea Islands. Gradually, people began to settle in Hawaii from all over. Now Hawaii is called the "_____ of the Pacific," with a large portion of its people being from Japanese, Caucasian, Filipino, and Chinese cultures.

   (a) Big Apple
   (b) Sunshine State
   (c) Melting Pot
   (d) Northern Lights

3. _____ is the capital city of Hawaii.

   (a) Honolulu
   (b) Polynesia
   (c) Tahiti
   (d) Tegucigalpa

4. The official bird of Hawaii is the Hawaiian goose, often called _____.

   (a) Mandarin duck
   (b) the nene
   (c) Mother Goose
   (d) Waikiki Poi

5. One of the natural specialties of Hawaii is the *lei*, or necklace of fresh flowers. It takes about one hundred _____ to make one average Hawaiian lei.

   (a) orchids
   (b) painted daisies
   (c) macadamia blossoms
   (d) ginger flowers

6. Among the specialties of Hawaiian craftsmanship are bowls and platters carved from the hard wood of _____.

   (a) giant redwoods
   (b) the eucalyptus tree
   (c) the monkeypod tree
   (d) the pandanus (hala) tree

7. Hawaii has given us its distinctive music, the hula dance, and _____, which used to be the sacred sport of kings.

   (a) polo
   (b) surfboarding
   (c) badminton
   (d) spear fishing

8. Hawaii has also given us the luau. *Luau* is a word that actually
   means the _____ that is used to wrap around some of
   the delicious food served at the Hawaiian native feast.

   (a) taro leaf
   (b) aluminum foil
   (c) plantain peel
   (d) cornhusk

ANSWER KEY:

1. b; 2. c; 3. a; 4. b; 5. d; 6. c; 7. b; 8. a

The main dish of the luau was customarily a whole pig, split,
filled with hot stones, and then buried in a pit surrounded by more
hot stones. Although preparations for our Luau Dinner are not
nearly so exotic, our results are every bit as impressive. Be sure
to allow a little over two hours from the time you begin until
dinnertime, but count on a good 40-minute breaktime.

Then call your family and friends to the table to enjoy sweet
and sour Island Spareribs, festive Kona Rice, and tropical Orange
and Avocado Aloha Salad. When you put the final touch on your
luau with our scrumptious Hawaiian Punch Parfaits, you'll have a
feast fit for King Kalakaua himself!

Island Spareribs   Kona Rice
Orange and Avocado Aloha Salad
Hawaiian Punch Parfaits

Island Spareribs

Succulent ribs baked in a marvelous sweet and sour sauce.

    4 to 4½ pounds spareribs
          3 tablespoons brown sugar, *packed*
          2 tablespoons cornstarch
          ½ teaspoon salt
          ¼ teaspoon ginger
          ¼ cup vinegar
          ½ cup ketchup
          1 tablespoon soy sauce
          1 can (8 to 9 ounces) crushed pineapple

1. Preheat the oven to 350°F.
2. Arrange the spareribs in a large, shallow pan with sides. (A jelly roll pan is a good choice.) Set aside.
3. In a medium saucepan, combine the remaining ingredients. Cook the mixture over medium-high heat, *stirring* constantly, until slightly thickened. (The cornstarch will cause the mixture to thicken as it is heated.)
4. When the mixture has thickened, remove it from the heat and carefully pour it evenly over the spareribs. Use a rubber scraper to remove all the sauce from the pot.
5. Set the spareribs in the preheated oven and *bake*, uncovered, for 1¾ hours.
6. Using potholders, carefully remove the pan from the oven. Use a serving fork to transfer the spareribs to a cutting board. Use a large, sharp knife to divide the ribs into serving-size portions. Place the ribs on a serving platter.

Kona Rice

Nuts and coconut make this dish special.

    ¼ cup (½ stick) butter
    2 cups uncooked converted rice
    5 cups water
    3 chicken bouillon cubes
    1½ tablespoons Worcestershire sauce
    3 green onions (scallions)
    ½ cup sliced almonds or macadamia nuts
    ¼ cup shredded coconut

1. In a large skillet, *melt* the butter over medium-high heat. Add the rice. Cook, *stirring* constantly, until the rice is browned (about 5 minutes).
2. In a large saucepan that has a lid, bring the water to a *rapid boil* over high heat. Add the bouillon cubes and Worcestershire sauce. Stir until the bouillon cubes dissolve.
3. Using a rubber scraper, carefully transfer the browned rice to the saucepan of boiling water, making sure to include any butter left in the skillet.

4. Bring the water and rice to a rapid boil and then reduce the heat and cover the saucepan. *Simmer* until the rice is tender and all the water is absorbed (about 25 minutes).
5. While the rice is cooking, rinse the green onions under cold water. Pat dry with paper towels. Use a paring knife to *cut* off the root ends of the onions. Discard these ends, along with any bruised or wilted parts of the onions. Thinly *slice* the onions, including both the white and green parts.
6. When the rice is cooked, add the sliced green onions, the nuts, and the coconut to the rice in the saucepan. Toss gently with a large spoon or fork to combine ingredients.
7. Transfer the rice to a serving bowl.

Orange and Avocado Aloha Salad

Be sure to serve this salad immediately or the avocado will turn brown, unless you coat the avocado pieces with some of the juice from the oranges or with additional orange juice.

1 medium-size head romaine lettuce
3 large navel oranges or 1 cup mandarin oranges, drained
1 large, ripe avocado
    salt and pepper to taste
    sweet and sour or celery seed salad dressing (your own or store-bought)

1. Rinse each lettuce leaf under cold water to remove any dirt. As you rinse, tear the lettuce into bite-size pieces. Discard any bruised or wilted leaves. Place the torn lettuce leaves in a colander to *drain*. Remove any excess moisture by patting dry with paper towels. Transfer the lettuce to a salad bowl. Cover with plastic wrap and refrigerate.
2. If using fresh oranges: *peel* the oranges. With your fingers, carefully separate each orange into sections. Remove the salad bowl with the lettuce from the refrigerator. Discard the plastic wrap. Place the orange sections (or mandarin orange segments) in a layer on top of the lettuce pieces.

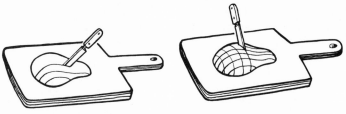

Dicing the avocado.

3. On a cutting board, use a sharp knife to *cut* the avocado in half *lengthwise*. Separate into 2 sections. Remove the large pit. Use the tip of the knife to pull off the tough outer skin from the avocado sections. Place the 2 avocado sections flat side down on a cutting board. *Dice* the avocado fruit by cutting lengthwise into strips, then *crosswise* into small pieces (see picture). Add the diced avocado to the salad bowl.
4. *Season* the salad to taste with salt and pepper.
5. Set the salad on the dining table and pass the salad dressing.

Hawaiian Punch Parfaits

Delicious!

   1 can (12 ounces) frozen red Hawaiian fruit-punch
     concentrate
1½ pints vanilla ice cream
 ½ cup macadamia nuts or shelled peanuts

1. Remove the unopened can of Hawaiian punch concentrate and the ice cream from the freezer to soften slightly.
2. Fill half of each of 6 parfait glasses with vanilla ice cream.
3. Spoon about 1 tablespoon of punch concentrate over the vanilla ice cream in each parfait glass.
4. Add enough vanilla ice cream to nearly fill each parfait glass.
5. Spoon an additional 1 tablespoon of punch concentrate over the top of each parfait. (Store the remainder of the Hawaiian punch concentrate in the freezer to use another time in parfaits or as a punch drink.)
6. If desired, add chopped nuts to the parfaits. Place the nuts on

a cutting board or in a wooden chopping bowl. Using a sharp knife, coarsely *chop* the nuts. Sprinkle the chopped nuts on top of each parfait.

7. Carefully place the parfaits in the freezer until dessert time.
8. At dessert time, remove the parfaits from the freezer and serve.

"LUAU" DINNER

Begin preparations about 2 hours and 10 minutes before dinnertime.

Phase	Island Spareribs	Kona Rice	Orange and Avocado Aloha Salad	Hawaiian Punch Parfaits
I	Steps 1–5			
II				Step 1
III			Step 1	
IV				Steps 2–7
40-MINUTE BREAKTIME				
V		Steps 1–5		
VI			Steps 2–5	
VII	Step 6	Steps 6–7		
VIII				At dessert time, Step 8

Glossary

Al dente. In Italian, "to the teeth." This is the point at which the pasta is just tender, but not soft. It is important not to overcook.

Bake. To cook food by dry heat in the oven.

Baste. To spoon liquid, such as melted fat, pan juices, and bouillon, over food while it is cooking. This keeps the food moist and adds flavor.

Beat. To mix food vigorously with a spoon, wire whisk, rotary beater, or electric mixer to thoroughly combine ingredients or to make the mixture smooth.

Blend. To mix ingredients together until thoroughly combined. Blending is more gentle than beating and is usually done with a spoon, wire whisk, or the low speed of the electric blender.

Boil. To heat liquid to 212° F., or to cook in liquid at 212° F. The surface will be a succession of bubbles, rapidly rising and breaking. There are three kinds of boils:
1. Rapid, or full and rolling: vigorous and fast bubbles
2. Medium: gentle, slow bubbles
3. Slow or low: barely above a *simmer*

Broil. To cook by exposure to direct heat in an oven, electric broiler, or on an open fire or grill.

Chop. To cut food in small pieces with a knife or food chopper.

Core. To remove with a paring knife or corer the core of certain vegetables or fruits, such as apples.

Cream.   To beat a solid fat, such as butter, margarine, or shortening, into a smooth consistency, using the back of a spoon or an electric mixer. Also, to combine a solid fat with another ingredient, such as sugar, until it becomes soft and creamy.

Crosswise.   Across, usually used to describe how food is cut; for example, cucumber slices.

Crumble.   To break food up into small pieces, usually with your fingers.

Crush.   To press with force, so as to break food into smaller pieces.

Cut.   To divide food into smaller pieces, using a knife or kitchen scissors.

Dash.   A small amount of something, usually seasoning, added to the food.

Diagonal.   On a slant, usually used to describe how food is cut; for example, celery.

Dice.   To cut with a knife into small, even cubes.

Dissolve.   To make a liquid solution by adding liquid to a solid substance, or by heating the solid substance until it melts.

Dollop.   A small amount of something soft, such as a spoonful of whipped cream.

Dot.   To place small amounts of an ingredient, usually butter or margarine, over food.

Drain.   To remove the liquid from food by placing the food with its liquid into a strainer or colander.

Flour.   To add a small amount of flour to a greased cooking pan or dish, and to shake the pan so that the flour sticks to the bottom and sides. Turn the pan upside down and tap lightly to remove any excess flour. (This helps to prevent baked foods from sticking to the pan.)

Fold.   To combine two or more ingredients (usually a lighter food into a heavier one) by cutting with a rubber spatula down through the center of the mixture to the bottom of the bowl, along the bottom, up the side, and over the top surface. This is repeated until ingredients are blended but still retain air.

Fork-tender.   Food can be pierced easily with the tines of a fork, such as when testing cooked vegetables for doneness.

Fry.   To cook food uncovered in fat in a frying pan.

Garnish.   To decorate or complement a dish with food that adds contrast in taste, texture, or color.

Grate.   To shred food or to reduce food to small particles by rubbing it against the teeth of a grater.

Grease. To rub fat (butter, margarine, shortening) onto the surface of cooking dishes, using a piece of waxed paper or a pastry brush.

Hull. To remove the stems from certain vegetables and fruits, such as strawberries.

Lengthwise. In a longitudinal direction, or the long way.

Medium boil. *See* **Boil.**

Melt. To heat fats and other solids until they become liquid.

Mince. To cut or chop into very fine pieces.

Mix. To combine ingredients by stirring.

Packed. To measure an ingredient, especially brown sugar, by pressing it firmly into a measuring cup or spoon.

Pare/peel. To remove the outer skin from fruits or vegetables with a sharp knife or vegetable peeler.

Rapid boil. *See* **Boil.**

Sauté. To cook in a small amount of hot fat, either just to brown or to cook completely.

Scorch. To burn slightly or parch.

Sear. To brown the surface of food rapidly with high heat, in the oven or over a burner. The term usually refers to meat.

Season. To add spices, herbs, or salts to food to make it more flavorful.

Shred. To cut food into slender pieces with a knife or shredder.

Simmer. To cook a liquid gently, just below the boiling point. There should be a few barely observable bubbles on the surface.

Skewer. A wooden or metal pin placed through chunks of meat, vegetables, or fruit to hold them in place for cooking or for decoration.

Slice. To cut a piece or pieces of food off a larger portion with a knife or slicer.

Slow boil. *See* **Boil.**

Stir. To mix ingredients with a spoon in a circular motion in order to combine them.

Stir-fry. To cook foods, stirring constantly, over high heat for a very short time, until just done. Meats should be barely cooked through, and vegetables should be crisp and unwilted.

Index